THE HISTORY OF THE INDIAN MUSEUM

THE HISTORY OF THE INDIAN MUSEUM

BY

ASUTOSH MOOKERJEE

GYAN

Published by

GYAN

Gyan Publishing House
5, Ansari Road
Daryaganj, New Delhi-110002
Phone: 011-47034999, 9811692060
E-mail: books@gyanbooks.com

Distribution Network
gyanbooks.com
India, USA, Canada, UK, Australia

ISBN: 978-93-6433-421-1 (PB)
First Published, 1914

2nd Impression 2024

Printed at: Gyan Press, Delhi.

THE HISTORY OF THE INDIAN MUSEUM
Author: ASUTOSH MOOKERJEE

The History of the Indian Museum.

An inaugural address delivered

by

The Hon. Justice Sir ASUTOSH MOOKERJEE, Kt., C.S.I., LL.D., D.Sc.,

Chairman of the Trustees,

On November 28th, 1913, in the Museum

Lecture Hall.

Calcutta:

Printed by order of the Trustees of the Indian Museum.

1914.

THE HISTORY OF THE INDIAN MUSEUM.

TO APPRECIATE the history of the origin and growth of the Indian Museum, we must travel back to the last quarter of the eighteenth century, when, after the establishment of British supremacy in this Province, Sir William Jones, one of the profoundest scholars, who have devoted their life to the service of India, founded the Asiatic Society in 1784, and with the boldness which characterized his genius, stated that the bounds of its investigations would be the geographical limits of Asia and that within these limits, its enquiries would be extended to whatever is performed by Man or produced by Nature. Sir William Jones, however, in his inaugural address did not expressly refer to the foundation of a Museum as part of the activities of the Society, which, at the time and for many years afterwards, had no habitation of its own. But curiosities sent in, from time to time, by members, began to accumulate, and in 1796 the idea was started that a suitable house should be erected for their reception and preservation. Donations were invited, but the plan proved premature, and it was not till the beginning of 1808 that the Society found itself in a position to occupy the premises erected at the corner of Park Street on land granted by Government. Six years later, definite effort was made to give effect to the intention to establish a Museum, when, on the 2nd February, 1814 Dr. Nathaniel Wallich, a Danish Botanist, who had been taken prisoner at the siege of Serampur but released in recognition of his scientific attainments, wrote a letter to the Society in which he strongly advocated the formation of a Museum and offered not only to act as Honorary Curator but also to supply duplicates from his own valuable collection to form a nucleus. The proposal found ready acceptance with the members of the Society, and it was determined to establish a Museum to be divided into two sections, one which would now be called archaeological, ethnological and technical, the other geological and zoological. The Librarian of the Society was placed in charge of the former section, while Dr. Wallich was appointed Superintendent of the latter. The scope of the Museum was defined in the widest possible terms, as an institution for the reception of all articles that might be sent to illustrate oriental manners and history, or to elucidate the peculiarities of Art or Nature in the East. Contributions were invited and specimens were solicited so that the Museum might include "inscriptions on stone or brass, ancient monuments, Hindu or Mahomedan, figures of Hindu deities, ancient coins, ancient manuscripts, instruments of war peculiar to the East, instruments of music, vessels used in religious ceremonies, implements of native art and manufacture, animals peculiar to India, dried or preserved, skeletons or particular bones of such animals, birds stuffed or preserved, dried plants and fruits, mineral or vegetable preparation peculiar to Eastern Pharmacy, ores of metals, native alloys of metals, minerals of every description," and other like articles serviceable to history and science. The Museum thus inaugurated thrived rapidly under the guidance of its enthusiastic founder Dr. Wallich, and individual collectors, amongst whom may be mentioned Col. Stuart, Dr. Tytler, General Mackenzie, Mr. Brian Hodgson, Capt. Dillon and Babu Ramkamal Sen, readily placed at the disposal of the Society interesting and curious objects collected from various parts of the country. After the resignation of Dr. Wallich, paid curators were appointed from time to time for longer or shorter periods on salaries ranging from Rs. 50 to Rs. 200 a month. In 1836, however, the Society, whose resources had, a few years earlier, been crippled by the failure of the bankers, Palmer & Co., found itself in financial difficulties and memorialized Government for a grant of Rs. 200 a month from public funds to enable it to meet the salary of the curator. The memorial, which was written by Sir Edward Ryan, then Chief Justice of the Supreme Court and President of the Society, impressively set forth the absolute necessity for the foundation and superintendence, quite as much for the furtherance of Science as for the instruction of the Indian fellow subjects of the memorialists, of a public depositary of the products of Nature in India and the surrounding countries, properly preserved, properly arranged, and properly applied. But, although the prayer of the memorial was limited to a grant of the modest sum of Rs. 200 a month, the Governor General in Council expressed their inability to accede to the request without reference to the Court of Directors, who were, as was pointed out, incurring considerable expense in keeping up a Museum and Library at the India House. It was conceded, however, that a Museum in this country could not be established by voluntary subscriptions nor maintained in the creditable and useful condition necessary for the attainment of the object desired, unless aided liberally by the Government, in like manner as similar institutions in Europe were supported from the public treasury. The members of the Society, however, were persistent in their demand, and presented a second petition for a temporary grant, pending reference to the Home authorities on the subject of the extension of the Museum and its conversion into a public institution; fortunately, this application was granted.

Dr. J. T. Pearson of the Bengal Medical Service was appointed curator and was succeeded, after a brief tenure of office, by the distinguished ichthyologist, Dr. McClelland. Meanwhile, the memorial of the Society for the formation of a National Museum at the cost of the State had been sent to the Home authorities, strongly supported and recommended by the Government of India. But the difficulties of communication in those days were so great that it was not till 1839 that the Government could obtain a reply from the Court of Directors in London. The Court sanctioned a grant of Rs. 300 a month for the salary of the curator and the maintenance of the Museum, and also authorized the Government of India to make grants from time to time for special purposes. Dr. McClelland, who had with great ability temporarily filled the office of curator, now resigned, and was succeeded by Mr. Edward Blyth, who had been selected by Dr. Horace Hayman Wilson in England. He proved himself ultimately to be an even more distinguished ichthyologist and naturalist than his predecessor.

Edward Blyth took up his duties as curator in September, 1841 and devoted himself to the duties of his new office with remarkable zeal; but as he was not a geologist, he found himself embarrassed in the management of the geological collections, which, at the time, were second in importance only to the archaeological collections of the Society. The difficulty of the situation was, however, successfully met by reason of the timely action which had already been taken by the Government of India. In 1835, the Government of India, encouraged by the satisfactory working of the coal-mines at Raneegunj and anxious to develop the mineral resources of the country (to which attention had been drawn by Dr. Helfer and other scientific officers), had decided to found a Museum of Economic Geology in Calcutta. This Museum was actually opened in 1840.

Shortly afterwards, in May 1841, Captain G. B. Tremenheere, who had been sent to England to secure a nucleus of a Museum of Economic Geology, returned to Calcutta with a large and valuable collection of specimens. These were deposited in the Society's rooms, and the Government of India sanctioned an additional grant of Rs. 250 a month for a separate curator. Mr. Piddington was appointed curator of the Geological collection inclusive of the specimens which were the property of the Society and which Mr. Edward Blyth had found it difficult to arrange. The Museum of Economic Geology thus constituted continued to occupy the premises of the Society till 1856, when the portion of the collection owned by the Government of India was removed and housed at No. 1, Hastings Street, in connection with the Geological Survey of India, then recently established. The Government, at the same time, expressed their readiness to receive the specimens owned by the Society; but this could not be done; for the Society, though fully alive to the fact that the collection was likely to be better preserved, better laid out and better taken care of by the members of the Geological Survey, refused to sanction their removal on the ground that the dissociation of a part of the Museum—and that the least expensive, highly valuable as it was—might not only prove injurious to the interests of the Society, but possibly postpone indefinitely the great object which the Society had cherished since 1837, namely that of seeing a national museum established here on a scale worthy of the Metropolis of British India.

The transference of the Museum of Economic Geology, however, immediately relieved to some extent the steadily increasing pressure on the limited space in the premises of the Society, and, for a short while, more room became available for the display of the archaeological and zoological collections. But the latter had grown with surprising rapidity under the able management of Blyth, with the enthusiastic co-operation of the members of the Society; and it became fairly apparent that their further growth would before long be arrested by reason as well of the restricted space as of the limited funds at the disposal of the Society.

In view of these circumstances, in 1856, the members of the Society decided to submit a memorial to the Government of India for the establishment in Calcutta of an Imperial Museum, to which they expressed their readiness to transfer all their extensive collections except their library. The dark days of the Mutiny, however, most inauspiciously intervened, and the consideration of the proposal was necessarily postponed. Two years later, the question was revived and a representation was submitted to Government in which the Society pressed for the foundation of an Imperial Museum at Calcutta.

The Government of India, though fully ready to recognize its duty to establish in the Metropolis an Imperial Museum for the collection and exposition of specimens of Natural History in all its branches and of other objects of interest, physical, economical and historical, declined to entertain the project on financial grounds. At the same time, the Government of India renewed its offer to relieve the Society by taking over the geological and palaeontological collections.

The members of the Society, however, were insistent and decided to memorialize the Secretary of State for India in Council. The effort was successful, and, in May, 1862 the Government of India announced that, in their opinion, the time had arrived when the foundation of a public Museum in Calcutta, which had been generally accepted as a duty of the Government, might be taken into consideration with regard to its practical realization. Negotiations which now followed between the Government of India and the Asiatic Society were protracted till the middle of the year 1865, when it was arranged that the Society should make over to the Board of Trustees for the proposed Museum the zoological, geological[1] and archaeological collections, and the Government should provide suitable accommodation for the Society in the Museum building, the portion allotted to the Society to be in their exclusive occupation and control. Legislative sanction was accorded to these conditions by the Indian Museum Act of 1866, and the valuable collections of the Society, accumulated during half a century by a long succession of enthusiastic members, were formally transferred to a Board of Trustees of which Sir Barnes Peacock, then Chief Justice of Bengal, was appointed President. The members included the Bishop of Calcutta, the Vice-Chancellor of the University and the President and three other representatives of the Asiatic Society. But although the negotiations had been carried on smoothly and harmoniously and had received legislative sanction, difficulties of a grave

[1] The geological collections were not transferred actually to the Trustees but to the Geological Survey.

order emerged as the erection of the Museum building made slow progress. It was realized before long that the building as planned could not possibly find accommodation for the Asiatic Society in addition to the Geological Survey and the Natural History Museum; it further became apparent that if the Asiatic Society were squeezed into the Museum building, its position as an independent body would be liable to be seriously affected. The Society consequently expressed its unwillingness to enter a building where accommodation was insufficient and freedom of action was liable to be cramped. The position thus created was one of great embarrassment, but the difficulty was solved by a committee consisting of one of the most sagacious administrators and one of the acutest scientists in the country, Sir Ashley Eden and Dr. Thomas Oldham. Upon their joint recommendation, the Government of India paid to the Asiatic Society a sum of one and a half lacs of rupees as compensation for its claim to accommodation in the projected Museum building. Doubts were expressed at the time as to the propriety of the course thus adopted, but after the lapse of nearly half a century, no one will venture to dispute that the arrangement has been highly beneficial to both the institutions and has fostered their growth and development.

We have now arrived at the stage at which the Museum ceased to be the property of the Asiatic Society of Bengal and was transformed into an Imperial Institution, but it was not till 1875 that the Museum building, one of the largest in this city, became ready for occupation.

As may be anticipated, the transference of the zoological and archaeological sections to the new building, and the arrangement of the specimens was a work of much labour and anxiety. This was successfully accomplished by Dr. John Anderson, who formerly held the Professorship of Natural Science in the Free Church College at Edinburgh, and was appointed the first curator on the 29th September, 1866, immediately after the Statute by which the Museum was established had been passed. A few years later Dr. Anderson's designation of Curator was changed to that of Superintendent, and he was also permitted by the Board of

Trustees to hold the Professorship of Comparative Anatomy at the Calcutta Medical College in addition to his duties in the Museum.

In the work of organization of the Museum in the new building, Dr. Anderson was ably assisted by Mr. James Wood-Mason. Dr. Anderson had foreseen, as early as 1867, that the assistance of a competent naturalist was essential to enable him effectively to arrange and organize the zoological section, and on his representation, the Government sanctioned an additional post of Assistant Curator, subsequently designated Deputy Superintendent. Considerable difficulty was at first experienced in the selection of a qualified assistant, but two years later, in 1869, the Trustees were fortunate to secure the services of Mr. James Wood-Mason, who had been selected for the post by Professor Huxley and Sir Joseph Hooker. Mr Wood-Mason proved himself a very capable and devoted worker and ultimately succeeded Dr. Anderson as Superintendent when the latter retired in 1886.

The exacting work of reorganization of the Museum upon which Dr. Anderson and Mr. Wood-Mason were engaged, occupied them for over two years, and thus, although the Museum building was ready for occupation in 1875, it was not till the 1st April, 1878 that the gallery containing the collection of birds and the archaeological gallery were thrown open to the public ; a few months later, in December, 1878 the public were admitted to the mammal gallery.

I shall not detain you with a detailed statement of the changes effected in the constitution of the Board of Trustees from time to time by the Legislature. It is sufficient to mention that in 1876 a new Statute was passed, by which the Statute of 1866 was repealed and the number of Trustees was increased from 13 to 16. In 1887 the number was further raised to 21 and opportunity was given to the Trustees to co-opt additional members. Finally, so recently as 1910, a new Statute was passed by which all the earlier enactments were repealed and the number of Trustees was fixed at 17. For the passing of this Act we are indebted mainly to the energy and scientific statesmanship of Sir Thomas Holland, Chairman of the Trustees from 1906 to 1909.

Three fundamental alterations in the constitution of the Board of Trustees were introduced by the Statute of 1910 and deserve special mention. In the first place, the officer in charge of each section of the Museum became a Trustee ex-officio, and was thus placed in a position to take part in the deliberations of the Trustees. In the second place, three members were allowed to be elected by Public Bodies, viz. one by the University of Calcutta, one by the Bengal Chamber of Commerce and one by the British Indian Association. In the third place, the number of representatives of the Asiatic Society, which by the Statute of 1866 was fixed at four and was raised to five in the Statutes of 1876 and 1887, was reduced to one. The effect of the changes thus recently introduced will, it is confidently expected, secure the more effective and harmonious administration of the Institution in the future.

I shall now pass on to a brief review of the development of the Museum since 1875, when the collections of the Asiatic Society were transferred to our new buildings. As already explained, the Museum, at the time, consisted, in the main, of the zoological, geological and archaeological collections. In June, 1882 the Government of India enquired from the Trustees whether accommodation could be provided in the Museum building for certain Economic products. The Trustees regretted their inability to accommodate such a collection, but expressed their readiness to favour an extension of the Museum building for the purpose suggested. Before effect could be given to this proposal, the Great Exhibition of 1883 was held in Calcutta. In 1884, after the Exhibition had been closed, it was suggested that the industrial collections, which had been brought to the Museum for the Exhibition, and under the designation of the Bengal Economic Museum, had been housed in temporary sheds on the site now occupied by the School of Art, might appropriately be amalgamated with the Indian Museum. The times were favourable for the acceptance of this scheme, which was rapidly advanced, and on the 1st April, 1887 the Economic and Art Section, which had formed a separate Institution under the direct control of the Government of Bengal, was placed under the Trustees, with Mr. T. N. Mookerjee, a recognized authority on Indian Artware, as the first assistant curator in charge of the new department.

The establishment of this new section at once made it essential for the Government seriously to grapple the question of additional accommodation which had been first mooted in 1882. The result was that in 1888 the construction of the wing in Sudder Street was commenced, and in 1891, Mr. Thurston, who was then officiating for Dr. Watt, the Reporter on Economic Products, found himself in a position to remove to the new building all the collections of economic products, artware and ethnology. The art gallery itself was opened to the public in September, 1892 and the ethnological gallery in January, 1893, but the economic court was not opened to the public till several years later, viz. in 1901, when Sir George Watt, the head of this section, retired and was succeeded by Mr. I. H. Burkill, now Director of the Botanical Gardens at Singapore.

The Museum which, as we have seen, had originally started with the zoological and archaeological sections, had thus had engrafted upon it, in course of time, the economic and art section, while the collections in the possession of the Geological Department occupied a somewhat anomalous and undefined position. The time had now evidently arrived, at which it was essential to secure the proper co-ordination of the institution as a whole and to ensure its harmonious growth in the future, that a comprehensive view of its scope and functions should be adopted. Consequently, in 1904 Sir Herbert Risley, then Chairman of the Trustees, proposed that the Museum might be divided into five sections, namely, zoological and ethnological, geological, archaeological, art, and industrial. This distribution ultimately received the sanction of the Legislature in 1910.

I have now dwelt briefly upon the history of the extension of the Museum buildings rendered necessary by the establishment of the new economic and art section. I shall pass on for a moment to a somewhat different aspect of our activities. As early as 1889, the need for extended accommodation for work and study rooms in the zoological and archaeological sections made itself keenly felt. A proposal to construct rooms on the roof of the main building was pronounced impracticable. Consequently, in 1891 the Board of Trustees pressed upon the Government of Bengal to fulfill their pledge to build an additional wing to the Museum, as it had agreed to do six years earlier.

Three years later, the local Government consented to provide for the accommodation of the offices, studies, laboratories, and store-rooms of the Museum and of the Geological Survey of India; this was accepted by the Trustees in satisfaction of all their outstanding claims. The building operations were commenced and carried on with a rapidity unknown in the annals of the Indian Museum, and in the following year the magnificent new east wing was completed and was available for use as soon as the internal fittings could be provided.

The pressure upon the public galleries meanwhile continued steadily to increase, and in 1904 a fresh scheme for the extension of the Museum building on the Chowringhee Road, which had been under prolonged consideration, took definite shape. The scheme was warmly welcomed by the government of Lord Curzon, and a handsome grant was generously provided to meet the cost of this extension. In 1911, this new wing of the Museum was practically completed, and its two lower floors were fitted up as public galleries; the top floor of the recently erected range is utilized for the offices of the art and the archaeological sections, while that of the old building is arranged for use as laboratories, as offices of the zoological section, and, finally as a lecture hall for the whole institution.

It is impossible within the time at my disposal to lay before the audience even a meagre account of the vast collections in the Indian Museum. But I must attempt a rapid survey of the various sources from which our collections have been derived. The zoological collections have been derived mainly from five different sources. In the first place, we have the original specimens collected by the

Asiatic Society of Bengal, mainly under the guidance of their energetic and devoted curator Edward Blyth. These possess an exceptional value as the original documents on which the descriptions of a very large number of Indian animals were based.

In the second place, we have the collections made by the Surgeon-Naturalists on board the Royal Indian Marine Survey Ship 'Investigator,' the zoological work whereof was initiated at the instance of the Asiatic Society of Bengal in 1875.

The first Surgeon-Naturalist was Dr. Armstrong who held the post from 1875-79, when he was succeeded by Dr. Giles. The latter was followed in 1888 by that distinguished scientist, Colonel Alcock, who subsequently became Superintendent of the Indian Museum. The 'Investigator' collection is of unique importance, as we have here specimens of the Abyssal Fauna of the Indian Seas, the majority of which come from depths varying from 100 to 1900 fathoms.

In the third place, we have the invaluable collections made in connection with official frontier expeditions. These include specimens obtained on most of the important military and political expeditions that have taken place during the last forty years on the Northern and Eastern frontiers of the Indian Empire, from the Persian Boundary Commission of 1870 to the Abor Expedition of 1911. On most of these expeditions, a medical man was specially instructed to collect zoological specimens, and, with the exception of the Lassa Expedition (euphemistically called the Tibet Frontier Commission of 1903), the majority of the specimens collected have been deposited in the Indian Museum. It is a hopeful sign that on the occasion of the Abor Expedition, a zoologist was officially deputed to collect specimens and information regarding the fauna and anthropology of the country traversed.

In the fourth place, private donors, too numerous to be individually mentioned, have ungrudgingly enriched our collections; but I cannot allow the present occasion to pass without special mention of the names of two distinguished officers of the Geological Survey, whose contributions are of abiding value, I mean Ferdinand Stoliczka and William Blanford.

In the fifth place, we are indebted to several of our officers for the contribution of valuable specimens to our collections. Two of our Superintendents, Dr. Anderson and Dr. Alcock, accompanied military or political expeditions beyond the frontier as doctors and naturalists, the former on two expeditions to Yunnan in 1868 and 1875, and the latter on the Pamir Boundary Commission in 1896; while our Assistant Superintendent, Mr. Kemp, joined the Abor Expedition of 1911 in the sole capacity of naturalist. These scientific workers made the fullest use of their exceptional opportunities, and the collections thus secured have proved to be of unique value; while the increased facilities for scientific tours latterly afforded to the members of our zoological staff has helped us greatly to make notable additions to our collection, more particularly of aquatic animals.

When we turn to our geological collections,[1] we find that they have been derived mainly from two sources. We have, in the first place, specimens collected by the members of the Asiatic Society of Bengal in the old days, and in the second place, the specimens collected by the officers of the Geological Survey since its foundation in 1851. The history and development of this department have proceeded generally on the same lines as those of the zoological collections. But there is this fundamental difference between the two cases, that the geological collections represent the result of a continuous policy supported by a comparatively large scientific staff, and, as a consequence, the geological collections are even more adequately representative of the Indian Empire and its frontiers than the zoological collections. I must not, however, venture upon even a superficial survey of the contents of the geological collections, as that would practically imply an attempt to write a history of the operations of the Geological Survey of India during the last sixty years.

---

[1] In the Geological Section of the Museum the Trustees merely possess visiting powers, which they assumed in 1910.

We next come to our archaeological collections, which are of unquestioned value to every serious student of Indian antiquities. The most considerable, and possibly the most attractive, portion of the specimens still consists of the statues, sculptured stones, inscriptions and coins collected by the members of the Asiatic Society of Bengal or presented to that Institution by investigators in all parts of the country, before the establishment of the Indian Museum as a separate institution maintained from the public funds. Every student of Indian antiquities, who has in any degree made himself familiar with the contents of the "Asiatick Researches" and of the "Journal of the Asiatic Society," will recollect that the names of many early contributors are closely connected with the specimens lent by the Society to the Indian Museum and now located in its buildings. Of this distinguished band of contributors, the name of General Alexander Cunningham stands out pre-eminent; and to him we owe the removal and preservation of the Bharut Stupa Rail, now one of the finest and most interesting existing relics of early Indian architecture. It is only necessary to add that since the archaeological section was placed under the Director General of Archaeology in 1910, many valuable coins, statues and other objects of interest have been deposited in Calcutta; amongst these, possibly the most notable addition to our collection consists of two stone figures, of a bull and a lion respectively, which date from the time of Asoka, and now stand erected at the entrance to the Museum.

Before I leave the archaeological collections, I cannot but make a passing reference to our extensive collection of coins, many of them lent by the Asiatic Society of Bengal, which were first catalogued by Mr. C. J. Rogers and have only recently been exhaustively described [1] by such competent numismatists as Mr. Vincent Smith and Mr. Nelson Wright.

Our industrial collections also are of exceptional importance and form an extremely interesting group of objects. Some of these are specimens of industrial arts collected by

---

[1] At least one other volume of the recent catalogue is still to appear.

the members of the Asiatic Society; but, as I have already indicated, a substantial portion of these exhibits was transferred to the Museum only after the close of the Calcutta Exhibition of 1883-84.

Until quite recently, the ethnological collections also were included in the economic section; they comprise weapons, implements, clothing, and other articles used by the various Indian tribes and races, and also life-size models of typical individuals of these tribes which were carefully prepared on the occasion of the Calcutta Exhibition. Some of the models of mechanical appliances can be traced as far back as 1828, while a collection of Javanese weapons is said to have been presented to the Asiatic Society at an even earlier period by Sir Stamford Raffles, who was British Governor of Java in 1815. Perhaps the most notable single addition to this collection is the fine set of Indian musical instruments presented by our distinguished fellow-citizen Raja Sir Sourindra Mohun Tagore.

Finally, we have the art collections, which have a history entirely different from that of the exhibits in the other sections. Some of these were transferred from the Industrial Section as recently as 1910, but a very considerable proportion is the property of the Government of Bengal and owe their preservation to the energy and enthusiasm of successive Principals of the Calcutta School of Art; this observation applies with special appropriateness to the pictures, which were selected principally by Mr. E. B. Havell and Mr. Percy Brown.

There is only one other aspect of our activities to which I propose to invite your attention, namely, the distinguished part taken by this institution in the noble cause of the advancement of knowledge. It would be difficult to overestimate the importance of the biological and geological research strenuously carried out by our officers, though it is by no means easy to assign, except in the case of zoology, the precise share of credit for such work to the Indian Museum as distinct from the related scientific departments of Government. It may be maintained, without risk of contradiction, that all the research work not only in zoology and geology but also in meteorology and archaeology, now undertaken by different Government Departments, owes its origin in the activities of the Asiatic Society of Bengal, and for many years the Museum in the rooms of the Society was the chief centre of such work in this country. The study and investigation of Applied Science, more particularly Botany and Chemistry, also had a similar origin.

The history of the development of the different sections of the Museum, since they came under our control, has, however, been so varied that it is only in zoology that it is possible to establish a claim for anything approaching a monopoly for the Indian Museum. The geological section, from the time of the foundation of the Geological Survey, has been incorporated therewith; the economic or industrial section has always been associated with the office of the Reporter on Economic Products to the Government of India, or, as he is now designated, the Economic Botanist to the Botanical Survey; the archaeological collections have been lent to the Director General of Archaeology in India.

The zoological section, on the other hand, has never been amalgamated at any time with an Imperial Survey Department, though we are now within measurable distance of the official recognition of the undoubted claims of zoology as a science pre-eminently useful and important, and of the foundation at no distant date of an Imperial Zoological Survey. The result of the position thus accidentally held in the past by the zoological section has been that the research work accomplished by our officers in this department is embodied in the long series of monographs and in the periodical publications issued by the Trustees of the Indian Museum. The "Records of the Indian Museum," which constitutes a Journal of Indian Zoology, has now reached its ninth volume, while the "Memoirs," of which four volumes have been hitherto published, include many original papers of first-rate importance, embodying the result of much patient and laborious investigation. The highly technical nature of these publications has served effectually to conceal their contents from the public, who are apt to judge of the importance of a Museum solely from the specimens exhibited in the public galleries; but it is a source of legitimate pride and satisfaction to all interested in the future development of our work that the excellence of the original investigations carried out by our officers has spread the reputation of this Institution far and wide, into every centre where the knowledge of zoology is cultivated, and its claims as a science fittingly recognized.

I have now placed before you what, I am afraid, cannot but be described as a somewhat imperfect history of the foundation and growth of the Indian Museum; I have narrated to you, how a century ago a small band of scholars, engaged in the study of the history, languages and antiquities of this country and determined upon the investigation of its natural products, laid the foundation for a Museum in this city, entirely with the limited private means at their disposal; how it took the ruling authorities thirty years to realize their undoubted responsibilities in this direction, notwithstanding persistent and oft-repeated reminders; and how once the duties of the Government in this matter were fully appreciated, arrangements were readily made for the establishment and gradual development of an Imperial Museum worthy of the Metropolis of the Indian Empire.

I naturally feel tempted at this stage to ask myself, whether the institution thus founded, developed, and nurtured has fulfilled its mission. I have no desire on the present occasion to enter upon an exhaustive discussion of the true functions of a Museum in relation to the community at large; but a brief consideration of the question may not be entirely useless. It is now generally recognized that a Museum is an institution for the preservation of those objects which best illustrate the phenomena of Nature and the works of Man, for the utilization of these in the increase of knowledge, and for the culture and enlightenment of the people. A National or Imperial Museum must, consequently, be equipped adequately for the fulfilment of three principal functions, viz. first, for the accumulation and preservation of specimens such as form the material basis of knowledge in the Arts and Sciences; secondly, for the elucidation and investigation of the specimens so collected and for the diffusion of the knowledge acquired thereby; and, thirdly, to make suitable arrangements calculated to arouse the interest of the public and to promote their instruction.

As regards the first two of these functions, the Indian Museum has no reason to reproach itself. We have taken adequate steps for purposes of record; that is, to preserve, for future comparative and critical study, the material upon which investigations have been made in the past, or which may confirm, correct, or modify the results of such studies. We have also taken measures for the advancement of learning, inasmuch as we have aided learned men in the work of extending the boundaries of knowledge, by affording them the use of material for investigation, laboratories, libraries and appliances. Nor have we been slow to stimulate original work in connection with our own collections and to promote the publication of the results reached by our investigators.

But I regret to confess, with a feeling of disappointment, that when I examine the history of the Indian Museum from the point of view of its third function as a possible powerful instrument for the instruction of the public, I cannot say that the fullest measure of success has been achieved. In so far as this third function is concerned, the Museum may be regarded, first, as an adjunct to the class room and the lecture room; secondly, as a bureau of information; and thirdly, as an institution for the culture of the people. A considerable measure of successful work has been accomplished in each of these directions, within the limited means at our disposal; but these aims are matters of vital importance for the promotion of which further determined effort must be made.

If we desire to furnish to the advanced or professional student, materials and opportunity for laboratory training; if we desire to aid the teacher of elementary, secondary, or technological knowledge in expounding to his pupils the principles of Art, Nature and History; our scientific staff must be materially strengthened; it would be disastrous to the success of the Indian Museum as an instrument for the

Advancement of Learning if our officers were seduced from their legitimate work of extending the boundaries of knowledge.

Again, it is unquestionably our duty to do our best for the culture of the public, through the display of attractive exhibition-series, well-planned, complete, and accurately labelled; and thus to stimulate and broaden the minds of those who are not engaged in scholarly research.

Here also, for lack of funds, we have not been able to arrange our public galleries as effectively as those of the great Museums of England, America and other civilized countries. But I am bound to observe that the extent of our effort in this direction has not always been correctly appreciated, and the numerous guide-books which have been prepared from time to time with considerable labour, have not very often received the recognition they deserve. I desire, consequently, to emphasize the urgent need for the improvement of our public galleries, and, generally, for the adoption of all necessary means to enable us to fulfil adequately our function as one of the most powerful agencies for the culture of the public and for the instruction of the advanced or professional student. For this purpose, we can confidently claim the assistance, not merely of the Government, but also of the generous and enlightened aristocracy throughout the country. It is not creditable to us that the Indian Museum should occupy the singular position of a great institution of which the paramount claims upon the community at large should scarcely if ever have been duly recognized. We have never lacked a constant succession of distinguished workers, and it is a matter of legitimate pride and satisfaction to all of us that the interests of the Museum are entrusted to a band of devoted and enthusiastic investigators, amongst whom we are at present able to count scholars of the stamp of Mr. Hayden, Mr. Hooper, Dr. Spooner, Mr. Percy Brown, Major Gage, and last but not least Dr. Annandale, who has been most unfalteringly jealous to maintain the high tradition of the institution.

The accomplishment of our work is safe in their hands; what they require is adequate funds for the full development of the institution, as also genuine recognition of their labours, not only by the State but also by the educated and cultured public.

CATALOGUE

of the

Exhibition prepared in connection with the Centenary Celebrations.

January 17th, 1914.

CATALOGUE OF THE CENTENARY EXHIBITION.

The following pages have been compiled to act as a guide to the special exhibition organized for the Centenary of the Indian Museum.

This exhibition has been formed almost exclusively by selection from the possessions of the Museum; it has had three principal aims:—(1) to explain certain lines of research recently pursued in the different sections, (2) to illustrate definite problems or aspects of history, art and science that could not be equally well illustrated elsewhere, and (3) to display some of the most precious and the most beautiful objects in the collections.

The several exhibits are classified as a matter of convenience under six headings:—

A. Archaeological.
B. Art.
C. Botanical.
D. Ethnological.
E. Geological.
F. Zoological.

A. ARCHAEOLOGICAL.

Exhibit No. I. Evolution of the Buddha Image.

Exhibited by the Archaeological Section.

Image worship is of comparatively recent origin in Buddhism. In the last centuries before Christ, Buddhists worshipped only relics and sacred symbols. Buddhist remains of these centuries show the absence of the figure of Buddha, even in the bas-reliefs which represent important scenes of the Master's life, whereas in bas-reliefs of a later period we find the figure of Buddha represented in such scenes.

A. The Gandhara School.

The Buddha image is to be found for the first time among specimens of the Gandhara School of Sculpture, also called Indo-Greek, Greco-Bactrian or Indo-Hellenic.

(See Foucher, L'Art Greco-Bouddhique; and V. A. Smith, A History of Art in India and Ceylon.)

The scarcity of inscribed images among specimens of the Gandhara School has made it difficult to trace the development of the school minutely, consequently it is seldom possible to date imagesof this school with accuracy. The figure of the Buddha is found both in the images and bas-reliefs of this school. At the same time we find that some of the images show the conventional postures of the hands (mudras), which in later schools of sculptures indicate particular incidents of the life of the Master. Thus we have the Bhumisparsa or Sakshimudra, the attitude of touching the earth, which is rather rare in this school, and represents the Sambodhi or the enlightenment of the Buddha; (Specimen No. 4900. See Bloch, Supplementary Catalogue of the Archaeological Collection of the Indian Museum, p. 14; and Foucher, L'Art Greco-Bouddhique, p. 402, fig. 203), or the Dharmmacakramudra, *i.e.* the attitude of turning the Wheel of the Law, which represents the First Sermon of the Buddha preached at Benares (Specimen No. 4838).

B. The Mathura School.

The art of the Gandhara School greatly influenced two other schools: (1) The Mathura School in the north, during the later period of its long development, and (2) The Amarawati School in the south. The Mathura School of Sculpture lasted for a very long time from the third century B.C. to the fourth or fifth century A.D. and according to some even longer, right up to the Muhammadan conquest.

(See Vogel, Catalogue of the Archaeological Museum at Mathura, 1910, and Annual Report of the Archaeological Survey of India, 1906-7, pp. 137–160).

The specimen exhibited belongs to the Gupta period (fourth or fifth century A.D.) and not to the Kushan period to which the earliest Buddha images of the Mathura School belong.

(Specimen No. M. 13. See Anderson, Catalogue and Handbook of the Archaeological Collections in the Indian Museum, Pt. I, p. 185). In this image the representation of the folds of the drapery is becoming stiff and formal.

C. The Amarawati School.

This school has been placed by Mr. V. A. Smith immediately after the Mathura School, and is the earliest school of South

Indian Sculpture. The specimen exhibited was lent by the authorities of the Madras Museum. It belongs to the period of the decadence of the school.

D. The Sarnath or Benares School.

This School of Sculpture rose into importance under the Imperial Guptas, and lasted till the Muhammadan conquest. Here we find that the simple and natural representation is gradually going out of use. The artists try to represent the ideal set before them in Indian literature. The specimen exhibited shows the artists of this school at their best. (Specimen No. S. 9. See Anderson, Catalogue and Handbook of the Archaeological Collections in the Indian Museum, Pt. II, p. 11).

E. The Bengal School.

Buddha images are rare in Northern India in the last centuries before the Christian era, except in the Eastern Provinces. In the Bengal School we find that each image represents a particular incident of the Master's life :—

(1) Specimen No. 5365.—Buddha in the earth-touching attitude, *i.e.* the illumination of Buddha.

(2) No. 3729.—Buddha in the attitude of turning the Wheel of the Law—the First Sermon at Benares.

(3) Specimen No. 6290.—Buddha seated on a snake, *i.e.* Buddha protected by Mucalinda.

(4) No. Kr. 5.—Buddha with Indra and Brahma, *i.e.* The descent from the heaven of the Trayastrinsas.

(5) No. 3773.—Buddha lying on a couch, *i.e.* the death or Mahaparinirvvana.

Besides these we have another class of images in which the main image is that of the Buddha in the attitude of touching the earth, while the seven other principal incidents of his life are represented on the back slab :—

(1) The Birth, (2) The First Sermon, (3) The Miracle of Sravasti, (4) The Taming of the Robbers, (5) the Taming of the Elephant or the Descent from the Heaven of the Thirty-three Gods, (6) the Presentation of Honey at Vaisali, and (7) The Death (Specimen No. 3737.—See Bloch, Supplementary Catalogue, pp. 46–47).

F. Buddha Images from Tibet and Further India.

The most ancient image from further India is that from Java (Specimen No. J. 5. See Anderson, Catalogue and Handbook of

Archaeological Specimens, Pt. II, p. 195). The principal characteristic of modern images of the Buddha is the elongation of the protuberance on the skull (ushnisha) which is round in Ancient Indian and Javanese images (Specimen Nos. 4737 and 4736 from Burma, No. 6310 from the Siamese States in the Malay Peninsula). Images from Tibet and later paintings found in the Central Asian desert exhibit the same characteristic.

Specimen No. Lk. I from Ladakh—Anderson's Catalogue and Handbook, Pt. II. p. 160.

Exh. II. Scenes of the Life of Buddha.

Representations of some of the principal incidents of the life of Buddha are to be found in bas-reliefs of the oldest School of Indian sculpture, *e.g.* the Conception, the Descent from the Heaven of the Thirty-three Gods, the Donation of the Jetavana in Bharhut Sculptures, and the Sambodhi, the First Meditation, the First Sermon, and the Donation of the Jetavana on the Bodh-Gaya Railing. But it is in the Indo-Greek School of Gandhara that we find representations of almost all incidents of the life of Buddha which are to be found in extant literature on the Buddha-Charita.

(See Foucher, L'Art Greco-Bouddhique du Gandhara, Paris, 1905, also Grunwedel-Burgess, Buddhist Art in India, and T. Bloch, Supplementary Catalogue of the Archaeological Collection of the Indian Museum, Calcutta, 1911). The specimens exhibited have been divided into four groups according to Mons. Foucher's classification.

A. The Cycle of the Nativity.

Specimen No. 5040.—Maya's Dream and its Interpretation.

Maya the mother of Buddha dreamed that a white elephant was entering her womb. The Buddha was conceived the same night. In the bas-relief, Mayadevi is lying on a couch, and a small elephant is seen, head downwards, above her.

Mayadevi told her husband, King Suddhodana, about her dream and he assembled a number of Brahmanas to interpret it. In the next compartment we find that the sage Devala is explaining the dream to the king and queen.

Specimen No 5034.—Buddha's Birth and the Seven Steps.

The queen was going on a visit to her own people, and on the way in a garden known as the Lummini or Lumbini she gave birth to the future Buddha. In the bas-relief Mayadevi is standing under the Sala tree and is holding a branch of it. On her left Brahma is extending his hands to receive the divine child on a piece of cloth. It is to be noticed that the future Buddha is issuing out of the left side of his mother. Below the hands of Brahma we find a child standing on the ground. This represents the Bodhisattva taking the seven steps immediately after his birth.

Specimen No. 5035.—The First Bath and the Return from Lumbini.

After the birth two springs of water appeared suddenly from the ground. The new-born child was bathed in this water after which the springs disappeared as suddenly as they came. In the bas-relief we find the child standing on a lotus (?) and being bathed.

In the adjoining compartment we find the representation of the journey from the garden to Kapilavastu. The mother and child are being brought back in a palanquin to the royal palace. The peculiar shape of the palanquin and the manner in which it is being carried should be observed. "The defect is due to the Western artist," says Dr. Bloch. "who created this type, an Indian palki was new to him; and, in order to show mother and child sitting inside it, he had to place them just in front."

Specimen No. 5041.—The Casting of the Horoscope.

After the return from Lumbini the king sent for astrologers. In the bas-relief we find the king and queen with the child and the sage Devala who is foretelling that the child will either be a mighty monarch or a Buddha.

Specimen No. G. 103.—The Birth of Chhandaka and Kanthaka.

On the day of the birth of the future Buddha a number of persons and animals were born who were to be associated with him in future. Among these were his charger Kanthaka and his groom Chhandaka. In the bas-relief we find the future groom being bathed in a tub and the colt drinking from another.

B. The Temptation and the Enlightenment.

Specimen No. 5050.—It is said that certain incidents of everyday life disgusted the future Buddha and he decided to leave his home. In the bas-relief we find his wife asleep on his couch and the Bodhisattva seated by her side.

Specimen No. 5045.—The Departure.

He then mounted his horse and left the city with his groom Chhandaka at dead of night. Nagaradevata or the city goddess opened the gates of the city for them. In the bas-relief we find the Nagaradevata with a mural crown on her head. The Bodhisattva is riding on Kanthaka and Chhandaka is holding an umbrella over his head. Two dwarfish figures hold the hoofs of the horse so that there might be no noise and the flight not noticed. The attendant figures are those of the guardian deities of the four cardinal points and Indra. Their presence indicates that the Bodhisattva is starting for the conquest of the world by means of the law.

Specimen No. 5047.—Dismissal of Kanthaka.

After proceeding a certain distance on horseback the Bodhisattva dismounted and dismissed his horse, which fell at his feet. In the bas-relief we find the horse kneeling on its front legs in order to salute the future Buddha.

Specimen No. G. 25.—The First Visit of Bimbisara.

One day the Bodhisattva was passing through the city of Rajagriha, then capital of Magadha, when he was seen by Bimbisara from the terrace of the palace. The king went to pay a visit to the ascetic prince and offered him everything that makes life agreeable, but the Bodhisattva refused to accept them. In the bas-relief we find that the king is kneeling in front of the royal hermit's seat.

Specimen No. 5052.—Emaciation on account of Austerities.

The Bodhisattva went to the village of the Kasyapas to the south of Gaya. There he began mortifications which became more and more severe, until he was reduced to a skeleton.

Specimen No. G. 18.—The Arrival at the Bodhi Tree.

When the Bodhisattva approached the Pippal tree, under which he was destined to attain perfect wisdom, a female appeared out of the tree to welcome him. This is seen in the bas-relief in which we see a seat under a tree and in front of it a human bust representing the deity of the tree.

Specimen No. 5053.—The Temptation and Attack by Mara.

Mara, the Satan of Buddhism, sent his three daughters to attack the Bodhisattva and on their discomfiture led an armed host to attack the future Buddha. In the bas-relief we find men in chariots, on horseback or on tigers going to the attack. The host is composed of all sorts of men with heads of tigers and buffaloes.

Specimen No. 4900.—The Defeat of Mara.

This armed host could not coerce the Bodhisattva and in the bas-relief we find two of them lying on the ground. Above them the Bodhisattva is seated in the attitude of touching the earth, which shows that the figure represents the incident of his perfect enlightenment. After the defeat of his party Mara is said to have approached the Buddha and asked him, "Who will be the witness of your perfect enlightenment?" On this the Buddha touched the earth, which rose at his call and became the witness.

It is interesting to note that the name of the Buddhist Satan, Mara, is equivalent to a snake in Persian; and in Christianity the snake is the symbol of Satan.

Specimen No. 5120.—The Presentation of the Alms-bowl.

After the defeat of Mara and Buddha's enlightenment, the guardian deities of the four cardinal points brought four alms-bowls and presented them to the Buddha, and he made them into one.

Specimen No. 5063.—The Invitation to Preach.

After his enlightenment the Buddha was requested to preach the true law to mankind by Brahma. In the bas-relief we find him surrounded by the gods.

C. The Ministry of Buddha.

Specimen No. 5054.—The First Sermon at Benares.

After his enlightenment Buddha meditated and found that his five former disciples were in the Deer Park at Benares : so he proceeded to Benares. The five disciples seeing him from a distance decided not to rise or salute him. But when he approached them the majesty of his appearance compelled them to rise. Buddha's first sermon was preached to them. In the bas-relief we find them seated on raised seats on each side of the Master. In front, the wheel, which is the symbol of the true law, rests on the triratna symbol, which in its turn rests on a pedestal. Two deers *sejant* at the foot of the pedestal shows that the event happened in the Deer Park.

Specimen No. G. 33.—The Serpent of the Kasyapas.

From Benares Buddha went to the residence of three brothers, Gaya Kasyapa, Nadi Kasyapa, and Uruvela Kasyapa, in order to convert them, and asked for permission to reside in the fire hall for the night. One of the brothers said that there was a snake in the hall which did not harm them as they were Arhats. Buddha went into the hall in spite of the warning, tamed the snake and put it into his alms-bowl and in the morning showed it to the brothers.

Specimen No. G. 9.—The Conversion of Uruvela Kasyapa.

After the incident of the fire hall the brothers became Buddha's disciples, one by one. In the bas-relief we find one of them seated at the door of his hut and Buddha standing in front.

Specimen No. G. 11.—The Ordination of Nanda.

When Buddha was on a visit to his own people he persuaded one of his kinsmen named Nanda to enter the order. Nanda was a young man and was loth to forsake his home and so fled. But he was brought back and influenced by Buddha to become a monk.

Specimen No. 5100.—Visit of Indra to Buddha.

Once while Buddha was seated inside a cave near Rajagriha, Indra came on a visit to him and asked him some questions, to which Buddha replied by writing on the floor. In the bas-relief we find Buddha seated inside the cave and Indra standing outside, his royal rank being denoted by the umbrella held over his head. On the other side the divine musician Panchasikha is playing on a stringed instrument—the Indian vina.

Specimen No. G. 16.—The Fright of Ananda.

Once Buddha was meditating inside a cave and his cousin Ananda was standing outside. Māra taking the shape of a vulture frightened Ananda. Buddha perceiving this from inside the cave put out his hand through the wall of the cave and patted Ananda on the head in order to embolden him.

Specimen No. G. 34.—The Episode of Rajagriha.

A householder of Rajagriha named Suka had invited the Buddha to his house. As Buddha entered a dog began to bark, whereon the Buddha told them that this dog in his previous birth had been one of the ancestors of Suka. He had amassed great wealth by his miserly habits and had died without performing any good deeds. In consequence thereof he was born as a dog and had been guarding the wealth, which was buried in the same house.

Specimen No. 2080.—The Miracle of Sravasti.

Some heretical teachers were arguing with Buddha and in order to vanquish them the Buddha made fire and water issue simultaneously out of his body.

Specimen No. 45105.—The Descent from Heaven of the Thirty-three Gods.

The Buddha had gone to heaven in order to preach the law to his mother. At the time of his return three ladders appeared leading from the heaven to the earth. Buddha descended by the central one and Indra and Brahma by those at the sides. At the foot of the ladders we find the kneeling figure of the nun Utpalavarṇā, who saw the Master first of all.

Specimen No. 5122.—The Taming of the Assassins.

Buddha's cousin Devadatta had tried to kill him by engaging some assassins. As Buddha was coming, the assassins lay behind the wall waiting to spring upon him. But when the Buddha arrived they were over-awed by the majesty of his appearance.

Specimen No. 2340.—Taming of the Mad Elephant.

Devadatta tried to kill Buddha by engaging the driver of a mad elephant to set it on him. As Buddha was proceeding along a street the keeper of the elephant let it loose, but the elephant on seeing the Master knelt down in submission.

D. The Cycle of the Death.

Specimen No. 5147.—The Buddha's decease at Kushinagara between the Śāla Trees.

In the bas-relief we see the last disciple Subhadra still meditating. In this specimen he is seated facing the front, but in some others his back only is shown. (Specimen No. 2543). On all sides we find Devas, Gandharvas and men lamenting the death of the great Master.

Specimen No. 5150.—The Burning of the Body.

The Master's body was dressed in new robes covered with flowers and burnt.

Specimen No. 2102.—The Coffin.

Specimen No. 5153.—The Worship of the Relics.

Specimens Nos. 5110 and 2583.—These show two different forms of the Triratna symbol. In one the three wheels denoting the three ratnas or jewels are piled together in the form of a pyramid, but in the other specimen we find the three wheels placed separately. This is the prototype of all later representations of the three jewels.

Exh. III. Bronze Images.

Bronze images of North Eastern India had considerable reputation before the Muhammadan conquest, but very few specimens have come to light as yet. The specimens exhibited, with one exception, belong to the Pala period of Indian History (800-1200 A D.). Three images of Visnu found in the Rangpur District of Bengal are among the best specimens of metal casting of the Eastern School. (Specimens Nos. N.S. 2249, 2250, 2251).

Specimen No. 4551.—The figure of Vajratara is an arrangement of Tara surrounded by eight other female figures inside a metal lotus which can be opened and closed. This and the remaining specimens were found in the Bhagalpur District. We have images of Ganesa, Bodhisattva Trailokyavijaya, the Buddhist Tara and a Sivalinga.

Specimen No. N.S. 77.—Visvarupa—A Brass Image from Nepal. 200 to 300 years old.

This represents a special form of Visnu with innumerable heads and hands. A description of this type of image has been found in the Gita.

Exh. IV. Inscriptions.

Specimen No. 5558.—A fragment of Asoka's rock-edicts at Mansehra in the North-West Frontier Province. This inscription was written in the Kharosthi script, which was written from right to left like modern Persian and Arabic.

Specimen No. 5984.—Eran inscription of Samudragupta—found at Eran in the Central Provinces, date 4th century A.D.

Specimen No. 5985.—Gwalior inscription of Mihirakula—this

is the only record of the Huna chieftain Mihirakula, son of Toramana, date middle of 5th century A.D.

Specimen No. 4104.—Garhwa inscription of Chandra Gupta II and Kumaragupta I, date first half of 5th century, written in the eastern variety of the early Gupta alphabet.

Specimen No. 2593.—Bodh-Gaya inscription of Mahanaman—date 588 A.D.—records the dedication of a Buddhist temple at Bodh-Gaya by a Ceylonese Elder named Mahanaman.

Specimen No. 4441.—Ghosrawa inscription of the time of Devapala—records the dedication of a temple by a Buddhist monk, who came from the monastery of Kanishka at Purusapura or Peshawar, to Bengal, and was elected elder of a monastery near Nalanda by the Emperor Devapaladeva. Date 9th century A.D.

Specimen No. 6262.—Nawada inscription of the poet Gangadhara—date 1137 A.D.—records an account of the imigration of Sakadvipi Brahmans, and of the family of the author, who is a well-known Sanskrit poet.

Deopara inscription of Vijayasena—date eleventh century A.D.—the only stone inscription of the Sena dynasty of Bengal. It records the dedication of a temple of Siva by Vijayasena; written in proto-Bengali characters.

Specimen No. N.S. 1.—Māṇḍā inscription of Gopala III—of the Pāla dynasty of Bengal—discovered by Babu Akshaya Kumar Maitreya, Director of the Varendra Research Society. Date 11th century A.D.

Specimen No. 6263.—Bodh-Gaya inscription of Asokachalla—date 117) A.D., it records the erection of a temple of Buddha at Bodh-Gaya by a king named Asokachalla in the 51st year of the era of Lakshmanasena.

Exh. V. Seals.

In ancient India seals were impressed on lumps of clay which were afterwards baked (Bloch, Annual Report of the Archaeological Survey of India, 1903-4).

The following seals were discovered at Basarh, the ancient Vaisali in the Muzaffarpur District :—

Specimen No. 6149.—Seal of Dhruvasvamini, queen of the Emperor Chandragupta II and mother of Kumaragupta I.

Specimen No. 6150.—Seal of Ghatotkachagupta, grandfather of Samudragupta.

Specimen Nos. 6151 to 6168.—Seals of Imperial Gupta officers.

Specimen No. 6177.—Seal of the Visnupada temple of Gaya.

Specimen No. 6176.—Seal of the temple of Siva named Amratakesvara at Benares.

Exh. VI. Votive Tablets.

It was a custom of Buddhist pilgrims to dedicate an image or a votive stupa at every place of pilgrimage. The richer class of pilgrims used to build temples and stupas; poorer persons had to content themselves with miniature temples and images, while the poorest used to purchase clay tablets bearing the impression of images or votive stupas. As Buddhism spread outside India, and the surrounding countries became well known on account of rapidly developing trade relations, numerous pilgrims began to visit India. At the time of their return from India they used to take away numbers of these little tablets of clay. A tablet with the representation of the temple at Bodh-Gaya was perhaps considered the most valuable (See J.A.S.B., N.S. Vol. III, p. 459).

Specimen No. 6295 is a tablet of the above description. It represents the temple at Bodh-Gaya and shows the big image of Buddha inside it. The next specimen (from Rangoon) represents the same thing. So do two other tablets covered with gold leaf, which came from some place in Burma. A small tablet from Arakan shows the representation of the thousand Buddhas, though the actual number is far less.

Two red tablets come from the ruins of a Buddhist monastery at Dharawat in the Gaya District and are the oldest votive tablets in this Museum (fifth century A.D.).

In 1908 five clay tablets found in the state of Trang in the Malay Peninsula were presented by Dr. N. Annandale; they formed a class by themselves as they bore representations of the images of the Bodhisattvas Avalokitesvara and Hari-Hari-Hari-Vahanodbhava-Lokesvara. Three of these seals represent Avalokitesvara Bodhisattva, while the fourth bears the figure of Buddha in the Dharmmacakramudra surrounded by eight other figures, one of which is Hari-Hari-Hari-Vahanodbhava-Lokesvara

The fifth tablet bears a figure of Tara. Another fine tablet bears a similar figure and seems to have come from further India but unfortunately its findspot cannot be ascertained.

Exh. VII. Coins.

I. The oldest form of Indian coinage was irregular in shape. The signati argenti of the historians of Alexander is no doubt the punch-marked coin, representations of which are to be found in the most ancient school of Indian sculpture. They are irregular pieces of gold and silver stamped with a number of different symbols, sometimes one over the other. Among these, the most ancient are supposed to be bent bars with a number of punch-marks. But the ordinary punch-marked coin is either irregular in shape or round. Roundness in a coin is rather unusual in ancient Indian Numismatics and has been attributed to foreign influence.

II. Indo-Greek Coinage :—

The oldest Greek coins of India are purely Greek both in shape and in type. After some time the Indo-Greek princes began to issue Bilingual coins most of which bear legends in Greek and Kharosthi. Only one or two specimens have been discovered which bear legends in Greek and Brahmi.

The earlier dynasty of Indo-Scythian monarchs copied the Indo-Greek types in their issues.

III. In the first century A.D. the coins of the Great Kushans show that Roman coins were being imported into India in very large numbers. The gold coins of the great Kushans show that their type was the same as that of the Roman aurei. Besides these some coins of Kadphises I are certainly copied from the copper coins of Gaius, grandson of Augustus.

IV. Assimilation of foreign influence produced the new type of Indian coinage after the rise of Guptas in Northern India Foreign influence both Greek and Roman began to disappear from it. The Kushan type of gold coin gradually became thoroughly Indian with the figure of king on one side and that of Sri or the Goddess of Fortune on the other. The exceptions are the Asvamedha type of Samudragupta, the horsemen type of Chandragupta II and Kumaragupta I, the king and queen type of Chandragupta I and Skandagupta, the lyrist type of Samudragupta and the lion slayer type of Chandragupta II and Kumaragupta I.

V. Sassanian influence on Indian Coinage.

From the seventh century onwards the coinage of the Sassanian dynasty of Persia greatly influenced the mediaeval coinage of Northern and Central India. The earliest Indo-Sassanian coins are no doubt those which bear Bilingual legend in Pahlavi and Sanskrit, *e.g.* Vahitiginadevanarita or the coins of the White Huns, Toramana, Mihirakula. Next to these are a class of coins found mostly in Rajputana and Southern Punjab generally called Gadhiya Rupees or paysa. Some coins attributed by Mr. V. A. Smith to Vigrahapala I of the Pala dynasty of Bengal are also copied from this type.

B. ART.

Exh. VIII. Metal Statuary from Nepal and Tibet.

Exhibited by Mr. Percy Brown.

Two cases, A and B, containing ten examples of metal statuary from Nepal and Tibet, selected from the collection of metal work in the Art Section of the Indian Museum.

The description of these specimens is as follows :—

Case A.

No. 1. PADMAPANI.

A copper-gilt figure of the Bodhisattva Padmapani, or Avalokiteshvara, "The Lord who looks down with pity," and the guardian deity of Tibet, of whom the Dalai Lama is said to be an incarnation; Padmapani is a divinity, who, under the supreme Adi-Buddha's command, creates all animate beings. The figure is entirely built up of hammered copper; the tiara and ornaments are set with rubies, turquoise, lapis lazuli, and crystals. The beautiful modelling of the hands is especially noticeable. The expression of the face suggests Mongolian influence, but the whole inspiration of the art is Indian, brought by Nepalese artists into Tibet about the seventh or eighth centuries A.D.

No. 2. TARA.

This charmingly graceful and spiritual Tara of hammered copper, gilt and richly jewelled, is a statuette of the Nepali-Tibetan School, and probably by the same hand as the fine figure of Avalokiteshvara.

It represents the Goddess of Transcendental Wisdom which leads to salvation. In Tibet this figure of Tara is worshipped in 24 different forms.

No. 3. MANJUSRI.

This figure depicts the Bodhisattva of Creative Science, dispelling ignorance with his uplifted sword of knowledge! It is a gilt copper statuette, and is interesting as an historical landmark, for the inscription on it in Nepalese shows that it was made to commemorate the death of a learned *pandit* and dedicated to a Nepalese shrine in the year A.D. 1782. It has all the fine sentiment and decorative skill of the older work, although the technique, more especially in the modelling of the lower limbs, is perfunctory, and cannot compare with some of the earlier examples.

Manjusri is also the Buddhist analogue of the Hindu Brahma, or Visvakarma. He is the great architect who constructs the mansions of the world by the supreme Adi-Buddha's command, as Padmapani by his command creates all animate beings.

Manjusri was the founder of Nepal. With his sword he cut a cleft in the range of mountains, which caused the lake to drain away and form the fertile "Valley of Nepal."

The full inscription, translated, is as follows:—"Blessing! Hail, Khagamaju! On the occasion of the death of Buddhacharya Ratna Traya this image of Manjusri was made in the Samvat year 902, month Kartika, 10th day of waning moon. Biss!"

No. 4. BUDDHA DORJE-CHANG.—THE SUPREME BUDDHA OF THE GELUGPA LAMAS OF TIBET.

A Nepalese copper-gilt statuette, representing Dorje-chang, the Lamaist counterpart of the Bodhisattva Vajrapani, "the Wielder of the Thunder-bolt," which attribute will be seen in his hand. It is built up of hammered work, but is comparatively late in date, probably not much more than a century old, representing the traditions of the Buddhist art of India which have survived in Nepal and Tibet to the present day. It has all the spirituality and true religious sentiment of Italian fourteenth and fifteenth-century art.

No. 5. Copper-gilt statuette of TARA, the goddess of Transcendental Wisdom. From Tibet.

Case B.

No. 6. Copper-gilt statuette of TARA, a goddess who represents the second of the ten forms of Mahavidya (Transcendental Knowledge). From Tibet.

No. 7. THREE LOOS OR WATER NYMPHS.

A very pleasing specimen of the work of the Nepal school, being a fragment of a scene evidently torn from some fixture in a temple. Three "loos" or water nymphs are rising out of the swirling current of the Ganges with the Himalayas in the distance. Above the peaks are conventional clouds, while grottos and passes are indicated running into the mountain range. The idea is a very beautiful one and the whole composition suggests the Rhine maidens of German legend, or some similar story.

No. 8. A BODHISATTVA.

A statuette cast in copper and gilt. The Bodhisattva holds in his left hand the *amrita* or Nectar of Immortality, while above is a graceful conventionalisation of the bo-tree—(the tree of wisdom)—disposed around the figure in the form of a wreath. At the foot of the pedestal are the portraits of the three devotees who dedicated this image to some Nepalese shrine.

No. 9. MAITREYA.

A very fine statuette cast in copper, from Nepal, of a Bodhisattva, probably Maitreya, the coming Buddha, "the Loving one," preaching. The date of it is difficult to determine; the figure itself may be of the eighth century, or earlier, but the pedestal and aureole behind are possibly later.

No. 10. VAGRAPANI OR VISVA-PANI.

A reclining figure with two *saktis* or attendant powers. Nepalese; probably eighth century.

C. BOTANICAL.

Exh. IX. Vegetable products from the Abor Country.

Exhibited by Mr. D. Hooper.

ACONITUM sp. Specimens of the roots.

ACTEPHILA EXCELSA. The leaves of this tree growing in villages are used as tea.

CANARIUM BENGALENSE. Specimens of the crude and prepared resin presented by Mr. Kemp.

CUCUMIS MELO. Melon seeds.

CUCUMIS MAXIMA. Gourd seeds.

DIOSPYROS sp. Fruits.

FICUS ELASTICA. Ball of crude rubber made in the hills.

GARCINIA CAMPANULETA. Specimen of fruit.

GOSSYPIUM sp. Sample of Abor Cotton.

GYNOCARDIA ODORATA. A peculiar form of the seeds of false Chaulmugra.

LABIATE. Capsules and Seeds.

LAGINARIA VULGARIS. Fruit of the Bottle Gourd.

MARSDENIA TINCTORIA. The leaves form the blue dye of the Abors.

MORINDA TINCTORIA. The roots form the red dye of the Abors.

MUCUNA IMBRICATA. Seeds eaten for food.

NICOTIANA TABACUM. Seeds of Abor tobacco

ORYZA SATIVA. Paddy grown in villages.

ZEA MAYS. Maize grown in villages.

D. ETHNOLOGICAL.

Exh. X. Abor Ethnology.

Exhibited by Mr. S. W. Kemp and Mr. J. Coggin Brown.

The Abors, a Tibeto-Burman tribe who are still in the earliest stages of primitive civilization, inhabit the valley of the Dihang and some of its tributaries, where the former river, known to the north as the Tsango-po of Tibet, breaks through the great terminal ranges of the Eastern Himalaya, to take its part in forming the Assam course of the Brahmaputra. This extensive collection of objects from the Abor country was made during the course of the punitive operations against the tribe in 1911-12. It is intended to illustrate the everyday life of the people and in it will be found most of their domestic utensils, ornaments, musical instruments, articles of clothing and weapons. As is only to be expected, artistic objects of metal, stone, or pottery are conspicuously absent, with one exception in the former case, —the large metal bowls which are used by the Abor as a form of currency. These are made in Tibet and are decorated with the northern Buddhist symbols of the wheel of life. They are only possessed by the wealthiest tribesmen and are but sparingly used on the most important ceremonial occasions, being kept safe under ordinary conditions by the simple but efficient process of burial underground.

The only ornamental metal work made in the country is seen in the shape of various bracelets, pipes, girdle and "boyap" discs. The "boyap" is a girdle of ornamented copper or brass plates worn by all young Abor women for a certain period of their lives.

Attention may be especially directed to the collection of hats, including the reinforced cane helmet of the warrior, which will easily turn an ordinary swordcut, to the curious palm-fibre waterproof satchel, and to the long swords, quivers, bows and poisoned arrows used in hill warfare on the North-East Frontier.

A collection of lantern slides, from photographs taken by Mr. S. W. Kemp, is also exhibited. This is intended to illustrate Abor types, domestic scenes in the villages and the wonderful tubular bridges which the Abor builds across the largest rivers.

E. GEOLOGICAL.

Exhibited by the Geological Survey of India.

Exh. XI. Characteristic Indian fossils.

Exhibited by Dr. G. E. Pilgrim, Palaeontologist, Geological Survey of India.

The case containing these fossils is arranged so as to show how a few of the characteristic forms of animal life succeeded one another in the world's history. The names placed vertically at the back of the case are those of the chief geological systems. Beneath these, representatives of the following great animal classes are arranged in horizontal bands: Trilobites, Ammonites, Bivalve Mollusca, Nummulites, Brachiopods, Mammals. The breadth and extension of the coloured bands on which the fossils are mounted represents the waxing and waning of that particular group of organisms. The particular fossil belonging to each group which corresponds to the geological system is eminently characteristic of that system, and any geologist, on seeing it, would at once be able to fix definitely the precise period at which the rock in which the fossil was found was deposited. The fossil specimens have in practically every case been found in India, and the labels give their names and localities.

Exh. XII.

Exhibited by Dr. G. E. Pilgrim.

This is a partial restoration of the lower jaw belonging to a remarkable carnivorous animal of an ancient type, which was found in the Lower Miocene beds of Baluchistan, and therefore lived about two million years ago. Its name is *Pterodon*, and it was probably the largest carnivore known. Beside it is placed for comparison the jaw of a modern Bengal tiger to illustrate both the difference in size and the way in which the modern carnivora have lost the greater number of their teeth. The fossil jaw has the full mammalian dentition of three molars, four pre-molars, one canine and three incisors. In the tiger, behind the canine there remain only two pre-molars and one molar. It may be noticed also how the first molar in modern carnivora like the tiger has usurped the entire carnassial function of the molars in ancient mammals.

Exh. XIII.

Exhibited by Dr. G. E. Pilgrim.

The specimens exhibited are arranged to illustrate two important principles of development: (1) The tendency of an organism to increase in size; (2) the existence of a sort of momentum which impels a peculiar feature, when once produced, to become accentuated far in excess of any possible use which it might be to its owner. The bottom left-hand specimen is that of the lower jaw of *Hyotherium*, a primitive pig in which the pre-molars have become disproportionately enlarged. This jaw occurs in the Middle Miocene, and above it are three other jaws which occur successively a little later up to the top of the Miocene, when the extraordinary animal called *Tetraconodon*, to which the topmost belonged, lived. No other mammal is known having pre-molars so out of proportion to the other teeth. These and perhaps other characteristics of which we know nothing no doubt put it out of harmony with the changing environment, and the particular type became extinct. On the right-hand side are placed for comparison three other jaws of ordinarily constituted pigs, one of them also occurring in the Middle Miocene and the gigantic one at the top of the Miocene. Gigantic pigs such as these were fairly frequent at that stage in the world's history, and their size was evidently their ruin, as they hardly persist beyond the Lower Pliocene.

Exh. XIV.

Exhibited by Dr. G. E. Pilgrim.

Several specimens of single teeth are here arranged to exhibit one of the most remarkable features which distinguish the teeth of modern ruminants from their predecessors of ancient times. This is their increase in length enabling a fresh grinding surface to be thrust up in the mouth to replace that which has been worn away. The types chosen are (1) *Orohippus* a small primitive ancestor of the modern horse, *Hipparion*, the three-toed horse, and *Equus*, the modern horse; (2) *Tragocerus*, a primitive goat antelope of the Upper Miocene, and the Tahr, the well-known Himalayan goat; (3) *Hemibos*, a primitive ox of the Lower Pliocene and a Pleistocene ox, *Bos*; (4) *Mastodon*, one of the

Miocene ancestors of the elephant, *Stegodon* and *Elephas*, the true elephant.

Exh. XV.

Exhibited by Dr. G. E. Pilgrim.

A fossil skull of *Tragocerus*, the Upper Miocene goat antelope, is placed side by side with one of the Tahr or Himalayan goat *Hemitragus jemlaicus* for comparison. We may notice that the horn-cores are very similar, but that the shape of the skull and in particular the hinder portion are very different in the two species.

Exh. XVI.

Exhibited by Dr. G. E. Pilgrim.

Hippopotamus was very abundant in past ages in India, and may have existed down to within historical times to judge from the resemblance of certain ancient sculptures to this animal. A skull of a *Hippopotamus*, with the rock in which it was found embedded attached to it, is placed for comparison with one which has been partially cleaned.

Exh. XVII.

Exhibited by Dr. G. E. Pilgrim.

A remarkable species of large oyster, which lives at the present day at the mouth of the Hughli, is here shown. The same species is known from the Miocene beds of Vienna, and a large bed of them was found a few years ago in digging the foundations of a house in Clive Street, affording evidence of the former estuarine conditions prevailing in Calcutta within comparatively recent times.

Exh. XVIII. Indian Zeolites.

Exhibited by Mr. J. Coggin Brown, Curator, Geological Survey of India.

The zeolite group contains a number of minerals which are usually hydrated silicates of alumina and alkalies, most of them also contain lime. Their water of crystallization is loosely held, and they intumesce when heated before the blowpipe. The lustre and crystalline form of the members of the zeolite group make them amongst the most beautiful of minerals, though they are of no commercial importance. They are found as decomposition products lining cavities in altered igneous rocks, having been mainly derived from the felspar; as a matter of fact some of the zeolites have practically the composition of hydrated felspar. The Deccan Trap of Western India has yielded some of the finest zeolites in the world, and exhibited in the case amongst others will be found the following specimens :—

STILBITE.—This is the commonest of our Deccan trap zeolitic minerals, next in abundance to it coming apophyllite, heulandite, and scolecite. It occurs both in crystals, which are often of large size, and are very commonly associated with apophyllite, lining drusy cavities in the trap, and in radiated lamellar masses entirely filling such cavities. One magnificent variety consists of large orange or salmon-coloured crystals, often two or three inches in length, usually compound or in sheaf-like aggregations, but occasionally in large flat prisms terminated by a four-sided pyramid.

APOPHYLLITE.—This mineral is sometimes not classed among the zeolites, though it is found under identical conditions with them. The Deccan trap has long been noted for the profusion in which apophyllite is found in it, and the beautiful crystals in which it occurs. In no other part of the world have equally fine ones been discovered. The best specimens were obtained from cuttings during the construction of the Bhor and Tekulghat sections on the Great Indian Peninsula Railway.

The mineral generally occurs in four-sided prisms with terminal planes, a form which closely resembles the cubical crystals of the isometric system, the double pyramid, with replacements of the secondary prismatic faces and terminal planes, so characteristic of this mineral in other localities, being chiefly typical of small crystals in the Deccan trap The colour of the Deccan apophyllite is usually white, more rarely pink or green, some crystals are perfectly transparent, and one of the most magnificent associations of minerals to be found anywhere is seen when, as occasionally happens, perfectly clear vitreous crystals of apophyllite, are inserted on a mass of orange stilbite. Some apophyllite crystals are as much as three or four inches across.

HEULANDITE.—The crystals of this mineral often have a characteristic coffin-shaped habit and a very pronounced pearly lustre along their well-marked cleavage planes. In colour they are white, pale salmon-pink, or red, and some of them are more than an inch long.

SCOLECITE —Remarkably fine specimens of this fibrous zeolite have been obtained from the tunnels and cuttings at the Bhor Ghat; in these it is associated with apophyllite and stilbite, and occurs in groups of radiating and divergent, transparent and semi-transparent, colourless crystals, some of which are over three inches long and nearly half an inch across; although, as a rule, they are thinner in proportion to their length. The exquisitely formed pyramidal terminations of these long acicular crystals are of the rarest occurrence and only seen on one or two specimens.

Exh. XIX. Machine for the Magnetic Separation of Minerals.

Exhibited by Mr. J. Coggin Brown.

The magnetic separator which is shown working, was made by the Humboldt Engineering Co. to specifications of the Geological Survey of India and is probably a unique example of its type.

Black sands, as they are called,—sands whose denser grains have been concentrated by the action of rivers or of the waves of the sea, more or less as a prospector washes gold in a pan to remove the lighter constituents, and leave a concentrate containing the heavy metal,—are very plentiful on the coasts of India. An important industry has lately been started on the southwestern shore of the Peninsula to exploit the valuable mineral Monazite, from which Thoria is obtained for the manufacture of incandescent light mantles; its high specific gravity accounts for its abundance in these sands. It is chiefly in connection with laboratory investigations of these Monazite deposits that the magnetic separator has proved its great usefulness.

The principle of its construction, due to Wetherill, is simple. A current circulates round the soft iron pole pieces rendering them temporary magnets, their attractive power being varied by altering the strength of the current. By means of suitable resistances it is thus possible to make the magnet attract to itself grains, let us say, of magnetite—which is one of the most magnetic minerals—leaving grains of similar size of all the less magnetic minerals unaffected. When the magnetite has been separated, the current may be increased so that the magnets are powerful enough to separate grains which are somewhat less magnetic than magnetite, ilmenite for instance; by increasing the current step by step in this way the minerals in the sand may be separated from one another in the order of their magnetism and are then available for further investigation.

The actual separation is affected by means of small conveyor belts of rubber. The unseparated sand grains are carried underneath the magnetic poles on one of these belts. Those grains, which are magnetic enough to be attracted, fly upwards towards the magnet. They are however not permitted to reach it, for on their way they are intercepted by striking the lower surface of another conveyor belt, to which they adhere until they are moved so far from the magnetic field that the magnets are no longer capable of sustaining them, when they drop from the belt into a suitable receptacle. Those grains which are unattracted by the magnets are carried undisturbed through the magnetic field and are collected in another receptacle.

Exh. XX. Minerals from Indian Pegmatite Veins.

Exhibited by Mr. J. Coggin Brown.

(The data given below are taken almost entirely from a memoir entitled "The Mica Deposits of India" by Sir Thomas H. Holland, K.C.I.E., D.Sc., F.R.S. Memoirs Geol. Surv. Ind., Vol. XXXIV, Pt. 2.)

Meaning of the Term.—The term pegmatite was originally proposed in 1822 by the French Abbé Hauy for the peculiar intergrowth of quartz and felspar now known as graphic granite; but in 1849 the term was extended in meaning by Delesse to cover coarse-grained veins containing silvery mica and often tourmaline, as well as quartz and felspar. The name thus became used to indicate the large size of the crystals irrespective of any peculiarity of structure, and lately its meaning has been used in a still more general sense to cover the coarsely crystallized varieties of other forms of plutonic igneous rocks like coarse-grained syenite, diorite, gabbro, etc., the variations in composition being indicated by the use of compound names, as granite-pegmatite, syenite-pegmatite, diroite-pegmatite, etc.

Origin of Pegmatites.—There is probably no other group of rocks whose origin has been the subject of more varied discussion than the pegmatites. It is now generally conceded that they have resulted from the consolidation of injected fluid magmas, often directly traceable to some large granitic mass. Recently, evidence has accumulated to show that the residual portions of granitic magmas, instead of being in a simple state of igneous fusion, contain much larger proportions of water than the average magma, and are consequently fluid at a much lower temperature. The injection of the aquo-igneous melt into the neighbouring rocks, or into fissures in the granite just solidified from the same magma, gives rise to the pegmatite veins.

Forms of Pegmatite Masses.—In India, as in other countries, the pegmatites are found associated with mica-schists, quartzites and other rocks of the Archaean group. Into these schists the pegmatites have been intruded, generally along, but sometimes across, the folia, in the form of thin sheets, lenticular bodies, or large, thick bosses. From sheets, uniform in thickness over large distances, we find various gradations down to small eye-like lenses, of which many may be found projecting from the schist surface over an area of only a few square yards, giving the impression that the pegmatite magma has thoroughly impregnated the schists.

Geographical Distribution.—Pegmatites are known at a very large number of places where the old crystalline rocks have been exposed in India. Presumably, large quantities of the same rock are also concealed by the extensive mantles of younger sedimentary strata and the great sheet of the Deccan Trap. Whilst the Himalayan range is composed of rocks which have been crumpled and sheared even since comparatively recent geological times, the Peninsula of India has remained as a firm solid mass since a very early period of the earth's history, and as a result many very old rocks, like the pegmatites, have been preserved with remarkable freshness. The pegmatite veins are commercially important owing to the mica which they contain, and India is able to boast of the finest mica deposits of the world. The known mica-bearing areas are given below.

BENGAL PRESIDENCY.—Gaya, Hazaribagh and Monghyr districts. Sikkim-Tibet.

BOMBAY PRESIDENCY.—Chhota Udepur, Narukot.

BURMA.

CENTRAL INDIA.—Rewah.

CENTRAL PROVINCES.—Balaghat, Bastar, Bilaspur.

COORG.

MADRAS PRESIDENCY.—Ganjam, Nellore, Nilgiris, Salem.

TRICHINOPOLI.—Vizagapatam, Travancore.

MYSORE.

PUNJAB.—Bhabeh, Gurgaon, Kangra.

RAJPUTANA.—Ajmere-Merwara, Jaipur, Kishongarh, Sirohi, Tonk.

Composition of the Pegmatites.—By far the majority of pegmatites are composed, like ordinary granite, of quartz, felspar and mica; but on account of the gigantic scale on which the crystals have developed, many comparatively rare minerals have been detected in them which have not been noticed in ordinary granites, possibly because of the small size of their crystals in the latter rock; others are possibly peculiar to pegmatites, and are due to the special conditions under which they have been formed. The following minerals, all of which are exhibited, have been noticed in Indian granite-pegmatites:—

Albite.—This mineral is one of the more important members of the plagioclase felspar group. It is a silicate of sodium and aluminium.

Allanite.—A complex silicate of calcium, aluminium and iron, containing the rare elements cerium, neodymium, praseodymium and lanthanum, and in smaller amount those of the yttrium group.

Apatite.—Pale green crystals of apatite, the phosphate and fluoride of calcium, have been found in several localities. In some countries this mineral is used as a source of phosphorus.

Automolite.—One of the rarer minerals of the spinel group, containing zinc.

Beryl.—Beryl, the silicate of beryllium and aluminium, in its pale green varieties, known as aquamarine, and the dark green varieties, known as emerald, is familiar to the world as a precious stone. The ordinary beryl found in pegmatite is generally in striated prisms without terminations, which often attain a great size, but are too full of flaws to be of any value as gems.

Biotite.—A dark coloured member of the mica group.

Lepidolite.—A rose or lilac coloured mica usually found in scaly aggregates. It is used in some parts of the world for the preparation of lithium salts, as it contains small quantities of this rare element. The chief use of lithium salts is in the preparation of mineral waters.

Muscovite.—Muscovite mica is the most valuable constituent of Indian pegmatite veins from the economic point of view, and it is of value purely because of the large size of the sheets it forms. Crystals or "books" of muscovite-mica have been obtained in Nellore district, measuring 10 feet across the basal planes, but usually, of course, they are much smaller, all gradations of size being obtained from those of marketable value down to scales of microscopic dimensions such as occur in the common massive granites. Some of the muscovite raised in the Hazaribagh district is noted for its red tint which in thick sheets may be a deep ruby colour. Amber-coloured, smoky-brown and, in one locality, deep grass-green muscovite is obtained in the Nellore district of Madras. The chief use of mica is for electrical purposes, it being employed as an insulating material in dynamos, motors, high voltage induction apparatus, switch boards, lamp sockets, etc. The use of mica for stove doors and lamp chimneys is decreasing. Scrap mica is used in the preparation of *micanite* or mica board which is sheet mica obtained by cementing small clear pieces of mica together under pressure. It can be rolled and bent and is utilized for the same purposes as sheet mica.

ORTHOCLASE.—A potash felspar. Some orthoclase shows the peculiar pearly opalescent appearance of the moon-stone and might be used in cheap jewellery.

PITCHBLENDE.—This mineral has been obtained from the Singar mica mines in the Gaya district. It contains uranium, lead, usually thorium or zirconium, and often the metals of the Lanthanum and Uttrium groups. It is exceedingly valuable as a possible source of Radium.

CASSITERITE.—Cassiterite or tin-stone, the oxide of tin, is almost the only source of that metal. It occurs in a pegmatite vein in the Hazaribagh district.

COLUMBITE.—Columbite is a member of a rare group of minerals known as the columbates and tantalates. They are mostly black opaque bodies, imperfectly crystallized and difficult to distinguish. Columbite is the most widely distributed and best crystallized of the group. It is a niobate of iron and manganese, in which a variable proportion of niobic is replaced by tantalic acid.. The metal tantalum is extensively used in the production of metallic filament electric lamps.

EPIDOTE.—A complex silicate of calcium and aluminium of no economic importance.

GARNET.—Garnets often occur in the pegmatite veins. In Bengal they are common enough and possess the correct colour, though they are rarely sufficiently clear, for the manufacture of cheap jewellery.

KYANITE.—A basic metasilicate of aluminium, often of a blue colour.

QUARTZ.—Quartz is one of the commonest minerals of pegmatite veins. It often assumes a beautiful pink or rose tint.

STAUROLITE.—A silicate of aluminium and a member of the epidote group.

TOURMALINE.—Tourmaline is a common accessory mineral in the pegmatite veins of Bengal and Madras. It is a borosilicate of aluminium and alkalies with iron and magnesium, containing also water and Fluorine. It possesses a sufficiently high specific gravity, hardness, and refractive index to make it an excellent gem stone; red varieties are known as rubellite; the indigo-blue variety as indicolite. Transparent green tourmaline and indicolite have been obtained in Bengal, but usually the mineral is of an opaque black colour and therefore useless as a gem.

TORBERNITE.—An emerald or grass green phosphate of uranium and copper, from the Singar mines.

TRIPLITE.—This mineral is a phosphate and fluoride of iron and manganese, containing about 32·2% of phosphoric acid. Though rare elsewhere it occurs in some quantity at the Singar mica mines in the Gaya district.

URANIUM OCHRE.—Orange and yellow decomposition products of Pitchblende or Uraninite are here classed under this general term. They are all radioactive and come from the Singar locality.

F. ZOOLOGICAL.

Exh. XXI. Deep-sea animals dredged by the R.I.M.S.S. "Investigator."

Exhibited by Major R. E. Lloyd and Captains R. B. Seymour Sewell and T. L. Bomford, I.M.S.

(See "Illustrations of the Zoology of the R I.M.S.S. 'Investigator'," etc.)

The present Marine Survey of India was established in the year 1874 for the purpose of making charts for the mariner's guidance. The Survey has also afforded an opportunity for a general investigation of the ocean and of the life within it. At first the work was somewhat limited, being carried on in boats and small vessels not specially constructed for surveying. In the year 1881 the first "Investigator," a wooden paddle steamer of 581 tons displacement, was built in Bombay and specially fitted both for survey work and oceanic research. The equipment included apparatus for dredging and trawling in great depths. Marine animals which have been discovered by these means are the subject of this exhibit. The work of preserving and arranging specimens collected by the ship has been in the hands of an officer styled Surgeon-Naturalist to the Marine Survey. The successive holders of this appointment, twelve in number, have been selected from the Indian Medical Service. Among them Lt.-Col. A. Alcock, F.R S., may be mentioned as the author of most of the descriptive work that has been published.

In 1907, the first "Investigator" was replaced by a vessel of modern type which retains the old name, and is at present engaged in a survey of the Mergui Archipelago.

A few of the more interesting deep-sea animals collected at various times by the old or new "Investigator" are exhibited.

FISH.

The conditions of life in depths of the ocean greater than 200 fathoms are peculiar. The superimposed water shuts out the heat and light of the sun and exerts an enormous pressure which increases with the depth and is of course in addition to the atmospheric pressure. The fish would not feel this pressure any more than we feel that of the atmosphere, since their tissues are adapted to withstand it; but when they are brought to the surface they gradually become distended and friable as the intense pressure of their normal environment is gradually lessened. Good specimens of deep-sea fish are therefore rarely obtained. Most deep-sea fish are black or bluish grey. In some, certain parts, such as the head, are white. Some of the Pediculati, a group of small frog-like fish, principally found in moderate depths, are scarlet or orange in colour.

Many deep-sea fish have special luminous organs, and it is probable that most are provided with some means of generating phosphorescent light, for although daylight does not reach them, their eyes are usually well developed. In some the eyes are unusually large enabling their possessors to see better in the dim phosphorescent light. Some have rudimentary eyes and we may assume from their general appearance that these blind fish spend their life wriggling in the soft mud which forms the bed of the ocean. The mouth is often very large being furnished with formidable teeth. In many the tail tapers to a point, a form seldom seen in shallow water fish.

The specimens selected for exhibition are as follows :—

Lamprogrammus niger. This is one of the commonest of the fish found in the depth of the Indian Ocean. Like most deep-sea fish it is black in colour. Well preserved specimens show a row of conspicuous scales along either side which are luminous during life. The surface of the head is peculiarly pitted. The tail tapers to a point.

LEPTODERMA AFFINIS. This species has been found several times by the "Investigator." It is dark slatey blue in colour. The eyes are large. The tail is pointed.

MACRURUS INVESTIGATORIS. The genus Macrurus contains many species which are widely distributed in the deep waters of the globe. The large eyes, small pointed snout and the filamentous tail are characteristics.

CHAULIODUS PAMMELAS. This species shows the large mouth and formidable teeth not uncommon in deep-sea fish. Rows of luminous organs appearing as white spots can be seen along either side of the body.

AULASTOMATOMORPHA PHOSPHOROPS. This species has only been found two or three times. The head of the fresh specimen is covered with pure white skin which is probably phosphorescent during life.

NEOSCOPELUS MACROLEPIDOTUS shows rows of luminous organs along the sides which are circular and concave like the reflecting mirror of a lantern. Many of the smaller deep-sea fish have luminous organs of this type.

CHAMSODON NIGER. A species not often found but remarkable for its ability to swallow other fish larger than itself.

RAJA REVERSA. The genus Raja, which includes the common skates of European seas, are rarely, if ever, found in the shallow waters of the tropics. But five species of this genus have been found in the depths of the Indian Ocean. In this species the upper surface of the body is white, the lower surface being pigmented. This arrangement of pigmentation is the reverse of that found in shallow-water rays. The upper surface was probably luminous in life.

BENTHOBATIS MORESBYI. This is closely allied to the electric ray or torpedo which it resembles in outward form. The eyes however are rudimentary.

CHAUNAX PICTUS. This fish is common in moderate depths, about 200 fathoms. It is pink in colour during life.

MALTHOPSIS LUTEA. Another fish from moderate depths, orange in colour.

BATHYPTEROIS GUENTHERI. This fish has rudimentary eyes, but many of its fin rays are lengthened and serve as feelers which have been compared to the blind man's stick.

CRUSTACEA.

Like the fish the Crustacea of the deep sea belong, for the most part, to families which are well recognized and have long been known among the fauna of shallow seas. Many of them are of a scarlet colour, a fact not easy to explain. The tendency to enlargement or reduction of the eyes is even more evident than among the fish. The following species are exhibited.

Aristeus crassipes. This is one of the commonest of the deep-sea Crustacea. Its resemblance to the edible prawn is evident. On more than one occasion specimens of this genus and of others have been seen to emit an intensely luminous fluid from two apertures in its head which correspond to the openings of the excretory organs in other prawns. It is probable that most of the large-eyed Crustacea from the depths possess this function.

The state of the eyes of the Crustacea is one of the most interesting facts to be observed among deep-sea animals. We may find two genera which resemble one another both superficially and deeply, in one of which the eyes are unusually large while in the other they are rudimentary. The following species should be compared with one another in respect to their eyes.

Munida andamanica and *Munidopsis triaena.*
Nephrops andamanica and *Nephropsis stewartii.*
Glyphocrangon investigatoris and *Plastocrangon caeca.*

The genus Munida is common in depths of less than 500 fathoms while Munidopsis is usually found in greater depths, but the two have often been taken on the same occasion from the same depths. Glyphocrangon and Plastocrangon are both found in depths greater than 500 fathoms. Nephrops lives in depths less than 200 fathoms while Nephropsis is usually found in greater depths.

Nematocarcinus cursor. A common deep-sea prawn with very long and slender legs. It probably lives in the water some distance above the floor of the ocean.

Homola megalops. A common deep-sea crab with large eyes.

Bathynomus giganteus. Belongs to the order of Isopods, which also includes the common wood louse. Bathynomus is by far the largest member of the order and is peculiar in possessing filamentous gills.

Scalpellum squamuliferum. The commonest representative of the barnacles or Cirripedia in the deeper parts of the Bay of Bengal. It is frequently found attached to the fibres of opal by means of which certain sponges anchor themselves in the mud.

MOLLUSCA.

Mollusca are found even in depths as great as 2000 fathoms. In many cases their shells are more delicate than those of shallow-water forms The antique genus Pleurotoma is very well represented in the deep sea. *Rostellaria delicatula* and *Pirula investigatoris* are very common about the 200 fathom line. *Xenophora pallidula* has the remarkable habit of fortifying itself with the shells of other molluscs.

ECHINODERMA.

This group includes the sea-urchins, the sea-cucumbers, star-fish, brittle-stars and sea-lilies. Many of the deep-sea forms are remarkable for their delicacy and for their peculiar outlines.

CORALS.

Deep-sea corals do not form massive reefs, but are remarkable for their beauty and delicacy of form. Many of them are the skeletons of solitary polyps resembling sea-anemones, or of small colonies of such polyps.

Exh. XXII. Remarkable Freshwater Invertebrates recently discovered in India.

Exhibited by Dr. N. Annandale, Mr. S. W. Kemp, Mr. F. H. Gravely and Mr. S. P. Agharkar.

(See "Records of the Indian Museum," Vol. II, pp. 211, 255; Vol. V, pp. 1, 197, 277; Vol. VI, pp. 219, 357; Vol. VII, pp. 113, 147, 205, 243, 283, 399; "Fauna of British India, Fresh-water Sponges, etc.")

SPONGES.

Corvospongilla.—This genus is remarkable for its hard skeleton, for the curious little birotulate spicules in its flesh and for the production, in many cases, of two kinds of gemmules, one adapted for floating, the other adherent to the support of the sponge. The distribution is Indo-African. Several recently described species are shown.

JELLYFISH.

LIMNOCNIDA INDICA.—The freshwater jellyfish or medusa of the tributaries of the R. Kistna in the Western Ghats was discovered three years ago by Mr. Agharkar. It is one of less than half a dozen true freshwater jellyfishes yet known and is very closely allied to species from tropical Africa and Rhodesia.

FLATWORMS.

CARIDINICOLA INDICA.—This curious little worm, which is related to one only known from Montenegro, belongs to the group Temnocephaloidea but connects this group with the Trematoda. It lives on the gills of small freshwater prawns of the genus Caridina and feeds on minute animals and plants which it seizes by means of a protrusible proboscis. Examples of the only other Indian Temnocephaloid (*Temnocephala semperi*) are exhibited for comparison. This worm adheres to the ventral surface of freshwater crabs. Caridinicola is widely distributed in India, while Temnocephala, which has a much wider general distribution, has only been found within the limits of the Indian Empire in Tenasserim and the Abor country.

POLYZOA.

VICTORELLA BENGALENSIS.—The little tubes that form an essential part of the individuals, and are joined together to compose the colonies, of this animal, constitute a fur-like growth on the stems of grasses, etc. The species is closely allied to forms found in Europe, Africa, Central Asia and Australia; it is only known from the Gangetic delta and from Madras and usually lives in brackish, only occasionally in fresh water.

PLUMATELLA TESTUDINICOLA.—The genus Plumatella is confined to fresh water, in which many of its species have a cosmopolitan distribution. This species is, however, only known from the Ganges. It adheres to the shell of aquatic tortoises and is modified in accordance with this mode of life in that its tubes lie flat and are pressed together in parallel lines to form an encrusting growth.

PECTINATELLA BURMANICA is one of the most massive Polyzoa as yet discovered, being surpassed in this respect only by the closely allied Japanese species *Pectinatella gelatinosa*. All the members of the genus are remarkable for the fact that young colonies are markedly gregarious and assemble in groups, having the power of independent movement. In older colonies these groups are embedded in a thick gelatinous substance probably secreted by minute algae which are invariably associated with them.

The species shown occurs in Burma, Ceylon and Orissa.

LEECHES.

Ozobranchus sp. The leeches of this genus are all parasitic on aquatic tortoises; the species exhibited is found on *Kachuga dhongoka* in the Ganges; it has not yet received a specific name. Like other members of its genus it possesses a series of plume-like gills on either side of the posterior part of its body. Other species are found on other tortoises in Ceylon and in the R. Mahanaddi, and yet others in Japan and other countries.

PARASITIC BARNACLES.

Sesarmaxenos monticola. The group Rhizocephala to which this animal belongs, consists of degenerate barnacles parasitic on other crustacea. In adult life they have no trace of limbs or mouth-parts but are merely sack-like bodies containing the reproductive organs, and as a rule broodpouches in which the larvae live for some time. With the exception of this species, which was found on a crab living in a hill stream in the Andaman Is., the whole group is marine. It is only by a study of the larvae that the true position of the Rhizocephala in the animal kingdom is known.

Figures of the larva and of the adult are shown, with specimens of a marine species for comparison.

LOWER FREE-LIVING CRUSTACEA.

Hyalodaphnia hypsicephala. A Water-Flea (Cladoceron) described by Prof. von Daday ("Allattani Kozlemenyek, X, 1911") from Bangalore. It is remarkable for its comparatively large size, in which it exceeds all other known species of its group, for its extraordinary shape, and for the fact that it occurs, apparently in all cases, in two forms or varieties, the difference between which is well shown in the photograph exhibited. One of these forms closely resembles a tropical African species.

Apus cancriformis.—This little crustacean is well known in Europe, in various parts of which large swarms occur occasionally in small pools of water. It has recently been discovered in the United Provinces and in Kashmir, in which it is said to appear annually in the flooded rice-fields and to devour the young rice. Specimens from Kashmir are very small.

PRISTICEPHALUS PRISCUS. Prof. von Daday described this species from collections made near Simla and in Kumaon. Like many other representatives of its group (the Phyllopoda), including Apus, it appears occasionally in temporary accumulations of water, its eggs being probably unable to hatch unless they have first undergone desiccation. Specimens of an allied form (*Streptocephalus dichotomus*) found in similar circumstances in different parts of India are shown for comparison. This animal was until recently known from a single specimen in the British Museum, labelled "Found in a can of milk, India."

FRESHWATER PRAWNS.

XIPHOCARIDINA ENSIROSTRIS. This little shrimp, belonging to the primitive family Atyidae, was originally described from New Zealand, but has recently been proved to occur also in parts of Assam. As it is not known from any intervening country, its distribution is most remarkable.

CARIDINA NILOTICA var. BENGALENSIS. Another little shrimp of the same family. It is common in brackish water in the Ganges delta and represents a local race of a species widely distributed, as a rule in fresh water, in Africa and Asia. Specimens of the typical form from Egypt are shown for comparison.

CARIDINA WEBERI. Various local races of this species, originally found in Celebes, occur in fresh water in different parts of India, Sumatra, etc. In India it is the common host of Caridinicola, which is also shown in this case.

PALAEMON LAMARREI. A representative of the family Palaemonidae. This prawn, which is very common both in fresh and in brackish water round Calcutta, was described as long ago as 1837, but was completely lost sight of until it was redescribed in 1908 by Dr. de Man. It has usually been confused with the much larger species *P. carcinus*, which is also common in this district.

PALAEMON MALCOLMSONI. Another common Indian prawn described long ago, but subsequently confused with *P. carcinus* and only reinstated in the last few years by Dr. J. R. Henderson and Mr. G. Mathai.

A specimen of *P. carcinus* is exhibited for comparison with these species.

Exh. XXIII. Recently discovered Freshwater Fishes of India.

Exhibited by Dr. B. L. Chaudhuri.

(See "Records of the Indian Museum," Vol. III, pp. 339–41; Vol. V, pp. 183–5; Vol. VII, pp. 437–44.)

The fishes exhibited here have been taken in the following districts :—Ambala (Punjab); Almora, Gharwal, Meerut and Naini Tal (United Provinces); Saran and Champaran (Bihar); Darjeeling and Jalpaiguri (Bengal) and Darrang and Manipur (Assam).

Of these, *Botia birdi* is to be noted for its size (the full-sized fish weighs up to 1½ lbs.) and *Botia lochachata* for its unique colouration. In *Nemachilus mackenziei*, a secondary sexual dimorphism has been noticed and described. The mature males of this species develop on each side of the head, in front of the eye, round cartilaginous flaps, the ridge above the groove often appearing slightly swollen and cushion-like. There is also a pad of thickened skin on the upper surface of the pectoral fins, and on it hooked denticular outgrowths of very minute size are often noticed. How far these male characters extend in the genus is not fully known. *Clupea suhia* is a freshwater herring and *Olyra kempi*, a catfish of remarkable form.

Exh. XXIV. The Freshwater Sting-Rays of the Ganges.

Exhibited by Dr. B. L. Chaudhuri.

(See "Journal and Proceedings of the Asiatic Society of Bengal," Vol. VII, pp. 625–9.)

These two sting-rays (*Trygon fluviatilis* and *Hypolophus sephen*) were first recorded from the Ganges by Buchannan (afterwards Hamilton) in his "Account of the Fishes in the Ganges" (1822), but his descriptions of them were imperfect and doubt was expressed as to their very existence by ichthyologists of later days. They were rediscovered in the bed of the Ganges between Burar and Rajmahal in 1910 and full descriptions were published. Proof was obtained at the same time that they breed in fresh water, and the young of both species were secured. These rays are thus proved to live and breed many miles above tidal influence, although both also live and breed in the sea.

Freshwater sting-rays are also found in the river Amazon in South America, but these belong to distinct species and genera.

Exh. XXV. Convergence in aquatic Animals.

Exhibited by Dr. N. Annandale.

(See "Memoirs of the Indian Museum," Vol, II, pp. 47, 64; "Records of the Indian Museum." Vol. VIII, p. 29; Vol. X, p. —; "Journal of the Asiatic Society of Bengal," 1913, p. 77.)

Convergence may be defined as a resemblance, either in general form or colouration or in the structure of particular organs, between animals that have similar habits or similar needs but are not alike because of a common ancestry. The exhibit shown in Case No. XXV illustrates this phenomenon in certain marine and freshwater animals.

(*a*) *Convergence in skeletal structure between different freshwater sponges*, viz., CORTISPONGILLA *from the Sea of Galilee and* LUBOMIRSKIA *from Lake Baikal.*

In both these sponges the external part of the sponge is provided with a hard crust or cortex formed of spicule-fibres and giving the sponge additional strength. In Lubomirskia, however, it is produced mainly by a profuse forking of the vertical fibres, whereas in Cortispongilla it is due rather to a thickening of the transverse ones. The former sponge belongs to the family Haplosceridae, the latter to the allied family Spongillidae.

Specimens of *Lubomirskia baicalensis* (Pallas) and *Cortispongilla barroisi* (Topsent) are shown, with figures of their skeleton.

(*b*) *Convergence in the form of certain spicules in different families of sponges.*

The type of spicule known as an amphidisc or birotulate has been evolved in the freshwater family Spongillidae from a simple rod-like form covered with spines, the spines at the two ends of the rod having become greatly lengthened and more or less completely fused together to form transverse crowns or discs.

In the marine family Desmaciodonidae a similar spicule has been evolved from a somewhat complicated type known as an isochela.

Again in the Hexactinellida, a very different group of marine sponges, a similar spicule occurs; but in this case its origin is not so clear.

Diagrams are shown illustrating the evolution of the gemmule-spicule in certain genera of Spongillidae and of the free birotulate spicule in other families.

(c) *Convergence in the degeneracy of calcareous plates in the stalked barnacles.*

The barnacles of the family Lepadidae bear typically five calcareous plates or "valves," the position and the general form of which are well defined, on the external surface of their capitulum; but these plates are all liable to become degenerate or to disappear, as a rule in accordance with a semi-parasitic mode of life. At least three different lines of convergent evolution can be traced in this respect:—

In different species of Poecilasma and Dichelaspis certain valves split in two, the two halves gradually separate from one another, take on a linear form and finally disappear; this evolutionary process is not accompanied by any marked thickening of the soft tissues. Most of these species live on the bodies of crustacea or sea-urchins.

In Conchoderma and Heterolepas some or all of the valves become small or disappear, without any tendency to split up, and the soft tissues of the capitulum become greatly thickened. The species of Conchoderma are often attached to whales and other marine animals; those of Heterolepas to shells, sea-urchins, etc.

In one species of Lepas (*L. tenuivalvata*), which is found on the skin of sea-snakes, the valves have almost disappeared on account, not of splitting or of reduction in size, but of the disappearance of calcareous matter from them.

The specimens and diagrams illustrate the process of degeneration, and the stages reached in different species on the three lines of evolution.

(d) *Convergence in the form of the shell between the marine oysters (Ostrea) and the freshwater family Aetheriidæ.*

The shells of the true oysters are adapted for firm adhesion to rocks, stones and the like, to which the lower valve of the shell is cemented, and their surface is rough and conspicuously laminated, giving them a close resemblance to inanimate objects as well as great strength. Exactly the same features are to be found in the shells of the Aetheriidae, a family of molluscs that occur in S. America, in tropical Africa and in India, in which they are represented by a single species (*Mülleria dalyi*, Smith) apparently existing only in the tributaries of the R. Kistna in Mysore and the Western Ghats.

Shells of this species and of the African *Aetheria caillaudi*, Fér., are shown, with true oyster-shells for comparison.

(e) Convergence in degeneration of the eyes in the Electric Rays or Torpedoes of Indian Seas.

The two commonest genera of Electric Rays in Indian seas are Narcine and Astrape. They are closely related to one another, but Narcine has two upright fins on the tail, whereas Astrape has only one. A deep-sea genus (Benthobatis) has been described by Col. Alcock which differs from Narcine chiefly in the degenerate condition of its eyes and in the comparatively feeble development of its lateral fins, the relatively great size of which is one of the most characteristic features of the rays as a group. The type species of Benthobatis has all the characters of an abyssal fish, namely a black colour, degenerate eyes and organs that probably produce light. A shallow-water genus (Bengalichthys) has, however, been discovered in the Bay of Bengal which, so far as the number of vertical fins and the degenerate eyes are concerned, bears the same relation to Astrape that Benthobatis does to Narcine; while its lateral fins are still further reduced, being relatively smaller than those of any other member of its family The size of the eyes and also the shape of the lateral fins are variable characters in most species of Narcine and Astrape, and in a deep-sea species of the former genus (*N. mollis*, Lloyd) the eyes are not degenerate. There is evidence, therefore, for believing that neither the degenerate condition of the optic organs nor the feeble nature of the lateral fins of Benthobatis is in its case due to life in the deepsea (although the eyes are reduced or absent in many deep-sea animals), but that these characters have been evolved independently in this genus and in Bengalichthys, in both instances in accordance with a life spent wriggling in the mud at the bottom.

The eyes are also degenerate in a Goby (*Gobioides rubicundus*, H.B.) that lives a similar life in the estuaries of the Ganges, and in the Indo-Gangetic Porpoise (*Platanista gangetica* (Lebeck)), which gropes for its food in the mud.

Specimens of Astrape, Bengalichthys, Narcine, Benthobatis and Gobiodon and a photograph of Platanista are exhibited.

(f) The independent evolution of pigmentation of the ventral surface in different deep-sea Rays.

It is well known that the ventral surface of most vertebrate animals is paler than the dorsal surface, and it has been shown in America that this type of colouration tends to concealment in natural surrounding. The Rays of shallow water are as a whole no exception to the rule, although dark spots and streaks occur on the bellies of some species (e.g. *Trygon marginatus*, Blyth) not found at great depths. In some deep-sea forms, however, the ventral surface is much darker than the dorsal surface (e.g. *Raja reversa*, Lloyd), while in many others (e.g. *Narcine mollis*, Lloyd, and *Benthobatis moresbyi*, Alcock) the back and the belly are equally dark. As these fish are not closely related to one another, but all differ in a similar manner from the majority of their kindred, it may be assumed that their dark ventral surfaces afford an instance of convergence. The peculiar colouration may be connected with the fact that the bottom of the deep sea is luminous. Its luminosity, reflected from the white belly of an ordinary Ray, would immediately alarm the bottom-living fish and crustacea, as their enemy swam along in search of prey, in the usual fashion of the Rays, a little above the bottom.

Narcine mollis and *Raja reversa* are represented among the fishes exhibited in the "Investigator" collection.

(*g*) *Convergence in general form between certain Carp* (*Cyprininae*) *of the Himalayas and Tibet and the Salmonidae or Trout.*

There are no true trout in the Himalayas or Tibet, but many of the Carp inhabiting, in these countries, what would be "trout-streams" in Europe have assumed a most remarkable, though quite superficial, resemblance to trout.

Specimens of the true Oxus Trout (*Salmo fario oxi*, Kessler) from Afghanistan and of the Tibetan "Snow Trout" (*Gymnocypris wadelli*, Regan), actually a Carp, are exhibited to illustrate this instance of convergence.

(*h*) *The independent evolution of adhesive suckers in different tadpoles and fishes inhabiting rapid-running streams.*

The newly hatched tadpoles of many frogs possess a little sucker on the belly by means of which they adhere to the remains of the spawn whence they have emerged. This sucker disappears early in larval development. In several species of Rana and allied genera (e.g. *R. afghana*) which inhabit the streams of the Himalayas a somewhat similar sucker is found in much the same position throughout the later larval life; it is different both in details of structure and in origin from that of the young larva. In other species of Rana that inhabit the same streamlets, the lips are greatly enlarged and are directed in such a way that they form a sucker-like organ precisely similar to that of *R. afghana* in function, though different again in structure and origin. The tadpole of the common Himalayan and

Burmese frog *R. liebigi* affords a good example of this lip-sucker. Other tadpoles are known from mountain streams in Eastern Asia that possess similar organs of adhesion; they belong not only to the family Ranidae, but also to the widely separated families Bufonidae and Hylidae; while in S. Africa a tadpole with a lip-sucker, but belonging to a fourth family (the Cystignathidae), has recently been described. In none of these families is the production of such organs common, and there can be no doubt that they have developed independently on different occasions in different regions and in different species.

Convergence of the same sort can also be traced in certain fishes of Himalayan streams that belong to the families Cyprinidae and Siluridae. In *Discognathus lamta*, which represents the former, the lips (more particularly the lower or posterior one) are greatly enlarged and form a sucker comparable to that of *Rana liebigi*; while in the Silurid genera Pseudechineis and Glyptosternum it is possible to trace what may be regarded as different stages in the evolution of a well-developed chest-sucker.

Specimens of the tadpoles of *Rana liebigi* and *R. afghana* and of the fish Discognathus, Pseudechineis and Glyptosternum, are shown, with figures of these and other sucker-bearing tadpoles and fish that have similar habits.

Exh. XXVI. The Invertebrate Fauna of the Sea of Galilee.

Exhibited by Dr. N. Annandale.

(See "Journal of the Asiatic Society of Bengal, 1913, p. 17, etc.)

The land fauna of the Jordan Valley and the fish of the river and its lakes are remarkable for their strong African affinities. These are, however, by no means conspicuous in the invertebrate fauna of the Lake of Tiberias (S. of Galilee), which may be regarded as an epitome of that of the Jordan system. The invertebrates of this lake, which is only about 13 miles long, are not (with the exception of the molluscs) prolific in species, and a larger portion of them are minute and unsuitable for exhibition. The selection shown in this case includes, therefore, only the more conspicuous forms.

SPONGES.

Five different kinds of sponges have been found in the lake, four having not yet been discovered elsewhere. Of these, three belong to a genus (Nudospongilla) that occurs also in Yunnan, Celebes and tropical Africa, while the fourth is the only known species of an apparently endemic genus (Cortispongilla). The fifth sponge is a local race of an almost cosmopolitan species.

POLYZOA.

Two representatives of this group have been described from the lake, one not known from any other locality, the other a local race of a widely distributed species (*Fredericella sultana*).

WORMS.

Three small flatworms of the genus Planaria have just been described by Mr. R. Whitehouse, while three earthworms (one of them first described a few months ago by Major J. Stephenson, I.M.S.) are common under stones at the edge of the lake. Specimens of this new species and of one common also in Europe are exhibited.

LEECHES.

Only two kinds of leeches have been recorded with certainty. One of these is a predaceous form that feeds on small worms, etc., and forms a local race of a widely distributed species (*Herpobdella* (*Dina*) *quadristriata*). The other is common in Eastern Europe and sucks the blood of tortoises.

Specimens of both are shown.

MOLLUSCA.

It is in this group that the invertebrate fauna is richest, and over thirty species have been described. Many of them are only known from the lake. The most remarkable feature of the molluscan fauna as a whole is the almost complete absence of thin-shelled species, although such species are not uncommon in the R. Jordan. This is probably due to the peculiar chemical composition of the water of the lake. A number of the more characteristic shells are shown.

CRUSTACEA.

The lower (and smaller) crustacea that form the bulk of the floating fauna ("plancton") belong to few species, none of which have any particular interest; the amphipods and isopods that live under stones near the margin are also inconspicuous. Of the higher crustacea (*i.e.* the crabs and prawns) there are only three species:—the Jordan Crab (*Potamon potamios*), the European

Freshwater Prawn (*Atyaephyra desmarestii*) and the Blind Prawn of Galilee (*Typhlocaris galilea*). The last is by far the most interesting of the three as it lives only in one small pool on the shores of the lake and is blind and colourless. Although thus apparently adapted for an underground existence, it does not shun the light of day. Specimens of the crab and the two prawns, and also of the plancton, are exhibited.

INSECTS.

The insects that breed in the lake or in the little springs and pools round it are interesting, chiefly because a considerable proportion of them are true Oriental species. Thus the three commonest mosquitoes at Tiberias are *Stegomyia fasciata*, *Anopheles culicifacies* and *A. palestiniensis* (=*nursei*), all of which are common in parts of, if not all over, India. The water-bugs also have strong tropical affinities and perhaps exhibit African connections more clearly than any purely aquatic group represented in the fauna.

Exh. XXVII. Type-specimens of Asiatic Squirrels.

The specimens shown are among the oldest specimens of mammals preserved in Asia. They are types of squirrels of the genus Sciurus and its ally Funambulus described by Blyth, Blanford and J. Anderson, and have recently been examined in connection with a catalogue of the Oriental squirrels, now in preparation by Mr. H. C. Robinson; they have been carefully repaired under his supervision in the Kuala Lumpur Museum. The oldest specimen selected for exhibition is that of *Funambulus layardi* (Blyth), which was mounted in the Asiatic Society's Museum 70 years ago. The specimens are exhibited to prove that it is possible to preserve mammal skins in Calcutta for an indefinite period, if proper precautions are taken, and also that the types of Blyth and other Indian zoologists of a comparatively early date are still in most cases available for examination.

Exh. XXVIII. Zoological specimens from the Abor Country.

Exhibited by Mr. S. W. Kemp.

(See Vol. VIII of the "Records of the Indian Museum").

The Abor country is situated to the north-east of Assam near the eastern limits of the Himalayas, from the foot-hills of which it extends northwards into the higher mountains. The expedition that entered the southern part of this country in the winter of 1911–12 was the first frontier expedition in Indian history that was accompanied by a zoologist in the sole capacity of naturalist. The specimens exhibited were obtained by him with the assistance of many military and medical officers.

MAMMALS.

No new mammals were discovered, but some of those of which specimens were obtained are of geographical interest, *e.g.* the squirrels *Sciurus stevensi* (described from the adjacent Mishmi country) and *Dremomys pernyi* (hitherto only known from Szechuen), and the gorgeously coloured Harlequin Bat (*Nycticejus ornatus*), which was described from the Khasi hills south of the Brahmaputra.

BIRDS.

The birds are mostly common Himalayan forms of no particular interest, but in several cases exhibit a tendency to be darker than usual. In one instance this tendency is so well marked that specimens have been selected as the types of a new race (*Rhipidura albicollis kempi*) by Mr. E. C. Stuart Baker, who has described the collection.

A fine male specimen of Beebe's Blood Pheasant (*Ithaginis kuseri*), previously known only from Yunnan, is shown with the Abor birds. It was taken by Capt. R. S. Kennedy, I.M.S., in the Mishmi hills.

REPTILES.

A large collection of reptiles was obtained. It includes the only known specimens of the peculiar little snake *Aproaspidops antecursorum*, which represents a previously undescribed genus, and of the much more conspicuous new species *Ablabes pavo*. Several other species taken by the expedition had not been previously recorded from any locality north of the Brahmaputra.

FROGS.

The Abor frogs are of very great interest; not only do they include a large number of new species, but they also prove that in certain respects the fauna of the foot-hills north of the Brahmaputra is distinctly Assamese rather than Himalayan. Attention may be directed to the extraordinary species *Phrynoderma moloch* and its tadpoles, which were found in water in a hollow log.

FISH.

The fish of the Abor hill streams include several species of particular interest, notably one representing a previously undescribed genus of loaches (*Aborichthys kempi*) and the curious little eel *Moringua hodgarti*. Specimens of one species (*Exostoma davidi*) only known previously from Tibet were obtained in these streams.

CRUSTACEA.

Several species of freshwater prawns, most of them previously undescribed, were found in the rivers at the base of the Abor hills, while the streams in the hills proved to be very rich in freshwater crabs, of which several new species and varieties have been described.

INSECTS.

The time of year at which the expedition took place was most unfavourable for the collection of most species of insects. A large proportion of those obtained were small and inconspicuous forms that lived under the bark of trees or under stones on the ground.

CENTIPEDES.

Only the larger centipedes have as yet been described. Specimens of an interesting new species are shown.

ONYCHOPHORA.

The representative of this small group (the members of which are often classed together under the name Peripatus) obtained by the Abor expedition was certainly its most important scientific "find," as none had previously been obtained north of the Isthmus of Kra in the Malay Peninsula. It has been described as a new genus and species by the name *Typhloperipatus williamsoni*. The Onychophora are intermediate in many respects between the annulated worms and the insects and their allies.

Specimens of several important groups (e.g. molluscs, earthworms and land planarians) cannot yet be exhibited as the work being done in connection with them is still incomplete.

Exh. XXIX. The Evolution and Distribution of certain Indo-Australian Beetles of the family Passalidae.

Exhibited by Mr. F. H. Gravely.

This exhibit illustrates a paper, read at the Science Congress, on "The evolution and distribution of certain Indo-Australian Passalidae."

Representatives of all the known genera of the strictly Oriental sub-family Aceraiinae, and of all but five of the known genera of the primarily Australian subfamily Gnaphaloonéminae, are arranged here in such a manner as to show the different modes by which an asymmetrical structure has been evolved in the head and mandibles of these insects; and the geographical distribution of the groups into which the insects fall when thus arranged, is indicated.

The exhibit is designed to show how much more closely related are the comparatively primitive forms of the two subfamilies now found (with one exception) only in Australia and Ceylon respectively, than are their more highly specialized representatives inhabiting only the intervening countries; and the way in which, in the Oriental Region, the centrifugal migration of the most highly specialized genus has been stopped by the Gangetic Plain, and that of another (a little less highly specialized) by the discontinuity of the jungle-clad hills of Southern India from those of Ceylon.

Exh. XXX. New Indian Diptera. (Two-winged Flies).

Exhibited by Mr. E. Brunetti.

The Diptera exhibited are not intended to be widely representative of the order as a whole, but merely to illustrate those families on which work has been chiefly concentrated during recent years in connection with the Indian Museum. The specimens shown all belong to species described since 1907; a representative selection of these species is displayed.

MYCETOPHILIDAE.

Many of the flies of this family inhabit mushrooms and fungi during their earlier stages and they are, therefore, called "fungus gnats" The larvae of some species are gregarious, that of *Sciara radicum* having caused much damage to lily bulbs in the Museum gardens. The majority of the species of this large family are harmless, occurring in woods and shady places, in outhouses and some on windows of buildings. They are mostly small or very small in size, obscure in colour and, comparatively speaking, somewhat lethargic in habits. Some of the Himalayan species are identical with those of Europe. Over a hundred Indian species in the Indian Museum have recently been described (Brunetti, "Fauna of British India. Diptera").

BIBIONIDAE.

A small family of harmless flies frequenting woods and meadows, and occasionally appearing for a few days in vast swarms, hovering rather heavily in the air or drifting with the wind. The sexes of the same species are often quite different in colour. Several new Indian species have been described (Brunetti, "Records of the Indian Museum," Vol. IV, p. 269).

SIMULIIDAE.

The term "sand-fly" is sometimes applied to these insects as well as to Phlebotomus. Though not numerous in species, the females cause infinite annoyance by their bites to both man and cattle, sometimes with fatal results. At times they appear in prodigious numbers. The Indian species ("Records of the Indian Museum," Vol. IV, p. 282) are found mainly in the hills, *Simulium indicum* being known locally as the "potu" fly. In their larval stages (aquatic) they are very interesting. The disease pellagra, common in many parts of the world, has been definitely attributed to the bites of Simulium, the only genus of the family. All the species are thick-set, short-legged, broad-winged flies of small size and with a characteristic venation.

PSYCHODIDAE.

Small, moth-like, hairy-winged flies. The members of at least one genus (Phelebotomus) often called "sand-flies," attack man, one species *Phlebotomus papatasi*, Scop., carrying "papatasi fever." Their bites cause much irritation. Several common species of Psychodidae occur in houses on windows. In Brunettia and Parabrunettia the wings are densely scaled, somewhat as in mosquitoes. The Indian species of Phleobotomus have been described by Annandale ("Records of the Indian Museum," Vol. IV, p. 35), and those of the other genera by Brunetti ("Records of the Indian Museum," Vol. IV, p. 289).

CHIRONOMIDAE.

Popularly known as "midges." About 200 species have been quite recently described from India by Prof. Kieffer ("Records of the Indian Museum," Vol. VI, pp. 113, 319; "Memoirs of the Indian Museum," Vol. II, p. 181) from types in the Museum collection. Culicoides is a genus that contains blood-sucking species. Most of the other genera are inoffensive, a few being actually beneficial as scavengers.

DIXIDAE.

A small group of harmless, graceful flies inhabiting shady spots, the life-history (aquatic) of some (European) species of Dixa, the only genus, being very interesting. The few Indian species (Brunetti, "Fauna of British India, Diptera") are exclusively from the hills and their habits have not been studied.

TIPULIDAE.

Known popularly as "daddy-long-legs" or "crane-flies." Numerous species occur throughout India, though they are more abundant in the Himalayas and other localities of some altitude. *Tipula carmichaeli* is probably the largest and handsomest species in the Orient. Most species inhabit shady spots, and many, especially the males, have a habit of aerial dancing under over-hanging boughs of trees. Some in the larval stage do considerable damage to the roots of grass; about 100 new Indian species were described recently by Brunetti ("Fauna of British India. Diptera").

RHYPHIDAE.

A limited group of delicate flies frequenting shady or moist situations, the few Indian species coming almost entirely from the hills.

STRATIOMYIDAE.

The Stratiomyidae inhabit marshy localities and have weak powers of flight. A characteristic of the venation, peculiar to this family alone, is the way the veins are crowded together in the anterior part of the wing. The commonest Indian species is *Sargus metallinus*, a bright metallic blue-green fly found on leaves. Very curiously formed species are known in this family, a further instance having been recently described, in *Monacanthomyia annandalei*, Brunetti ("Records of the Indian Museum," Vol. VII, p. 448). The Oriental species of the family have been revised by the same author in Vol. I, p. 85.

LEPTIDAE.

These inhabit woods and fields; *Leptis apicipennis*, Brun., is not uncommon at Darjeeling in autumn. Atrichops is a genus with prettily marked wings of which several new Indian species have been described.

TABANIDAE.

Generally known as "gad-flies," the females being a great torment to cattle and horses; the males do not bite. Many species are common in India, nearly 2000 existing throughout the world. One genus, Chrysops, is conspicuous for its prettily marked wings. Pangonia is easily known by its elongate proboscis. Many new Indian species have been described by Miss Ricardo ("Records of the Indian Museum," Vol. IV, pp. 111 and 321).

BOMBYLIDAE.

Some very large, beautiful, often hairy, bee-like flies belong to this family; the numerous Indian species have been revised and added to recently (Brunetti, "Records of the Indian Museum," Vol. II, p. 43 and Vol. III, p. 211). They hover in the sunlight over paths, under boughs of trees or in small open spaces in woods and are exceedingly difficult to catch. None are in any stage harmful.

NEMESTRINIDAE.

These also are hoverers, but rather sombre, innocuous flies with similar habits to those of the last family. Their venation is peculiar. The few Indian species (described by Herr Lichtwadt, "Records of the Indian Museum," Vol. IX, p. 333) occur only in the hills.

CYRTIDAE.

Curious, almost globular insects with unlimited powers of hovering. The venation varies in this small family more than in any other. Their larvae are parasitic on spiders or their cocoons.

MYDASIDAE.

A restricted group, comprising large, mostly black flies (often with yellow or red spots and bands). Innocuous; only five species are Oriental, *Mydas carmichaeli* and *Leptomidas indianus* being described but recently.

EMPIDAE.

Over fifty new Indian species of this extensive family of innocuous sombre flies have been described of late ("Records of the Indian Museum," Vol. IX, p. 11).

SYRPHIDAE.

Known as "hover-flies." Numerous handsome species of this very extensive family are Indian. Some of the Himalayan ones are identical with those of Europe, China and Japan. Many kinds occur throughout the greater part of the summer in sunny spots and on flowers.

None are injurious to man's economy and some species are actually beneficial. The habits of the larvae are very variable. The perfect insects exhibit great variety, except in the venation, which is remarkably uniform. Numerous new Indian species were described by Brunetti in the "Records of the Indian Museum," Vol. II, p. 49; the same author having a further paper on the point of completion.

CONOPIDAE.

Wasp-like flies, some of which occur sparingly throughout India. They are parasitic on wasps and bees and are in no way harmful to man.

MUSCIDAE.

Section I. Calyptrata.

The Muscidae, comprising the "house flies" and their allies, comprise nearly one half of the known species belonging to this order. The domestic species, of which there are a good number, are very generally distributed; they are abundant in individuals and are also great carriers of disease, especially the genera Musca (house-fly proper), Calliphora (blow-fly), Lucilia (blue bottle or green bottle) and their allies. The species of Musca are now beginning to engage the attention of medical men. *Musca eutaeniata*, Big., occurs sometimes in great numbers and becomes a great pest to cattle, attacking all abrasions of the skin. Several species of blood-suckers belong to this family. Stomoxys and Lyperosia have a powerful horny proboscis with which they attack cattle, whilst *Philaematomyia insignis*, Aust., found probably throughout the East, although unable to bore a hole itself, has a kind of circular saw apparatus in its trunk that enables it to enlarge a small hole already made and to suck the blood.

A kindred species, *P. lineata*, Brun., has lately been set up, and a revision of the Indian-blood sucking Muscidae is offered by Brunetti ("Records of the Indian Museum," Vol. IV, p. 59). All the domestic species already referred to breed in any animal or vegetable refuse heap and produce enormous progenies.

The Tachininae, one of the subfamilies of the Muscidae, pass their earlier stages in the caterpillars of butterflies and moths, and are of high economic value, from their check on the over-production of lepidopterous crop pests. They are conspicuous by the strong spines that invariably cover most of the body; many species attain a large size and some exhibit much variety of colour, but the eastern species have never been seriously studied.

The Anthomyinae, another Muscid subfamily, include many species that in early life are leaf miners, or live in the roots of vegetables, such as the genus Phorbia.

A large number of species are Indian, but still await a thorough revision. They are generally inconspicuously coloured, Limnophora and one or two other genera excepted. Lispa and Spilogaster have spotted abdomens in most of the species. Ophyra is a splendid hoverer in the sunlight under boughs of trees.

Section II. Acalyptrata.

Mostly small flies, some being of economic interest, such as the Trypetinae of which Prof. Bezzi has recently monographed the species of the Museum collection ("Memoirs of the Indian Museum," Vol. III, No. 3). Piophila is known as the cheese-maggot in its larval state; the Oscininae, an extensive group, affect cereals. Many genera frequent manure heaps, such genera being nearly cosmopolitan, *e.g.* Scatophaga, Sepsis, Drosophila, Limosina. It is highly probable that contagious diseases are transmitted by some of them. The Indian species of Sepsinae have been revised by Brunetti ("Records of the Indian Museum," Vol. III, p. 343).

The "eye fly" (*Siphonella funicula*, Meij.) is a great pest at times in Ceylon and in parts of India.

PHORIDAE.

An isolated group with uncertain affinities. *Aphiochaeta ferruginea*, Brun. ("Records of the Indian Museum," Vol. VII, p. 83), seems to infest the tropical regions of many other parts of the world as well as India. It probably breeds in any vegetable or animal matter and has been known to complete its life cycle as an internal human parasite. The family is easily recognized from all others by its characteristic venation.

Exh. XXXI. Exhibition Cases illustrating the morphology and biology of insects and their allies.

Exhibited by Mr. F. H. Gravely.

The five cases composing this exhibit form the greater part of a series, now in course of preparation for exhibition in the public galleries, to illustrate some of the more important features of the morphology and biology of insects, myriapods and arachnids.

The subject is dealt with under the following heads, to each of which one case, with a special descriptive label, is allotted :—

(1) External morphology of insects. The external anatomy of a grasshopper, a beetle and a bug is illustrated by disarticulated specimens. The structure of the mouth-parts of a cockroach, a bee, a fly and a bug is illustrated by means of diagrams.

The internal anatomy of insects is illustrated in the gallery by ordinary models, prepared commercially in Europe. These have been omitted from the present exhibit.

(2) Prototracheata Myriapoda, and Arachnida.

The anatomy of Peripatus and Scutigerella is illustrated by diagrams; and the external anatomy of a millepede, centipede, king-crab, scorpion, and spider by disarticulated specimens.

(3) The vocal and auditory organs of insects. Several of the different types of these organs found among insects, are illustrated by means of specimens accompanied by diagrams.

(4) Secondary sexual characters. It has been found convenient to divide insects exhibiting these phenomena into three main groups: (i) Insects in which the males have the organs used in searching for a female (antennae or eyes) specially enlarged, the power of flight in the female being in some instances correspondingly reduced or absent; (ii) Insects in which special characters are produced in the male, which are likely to render him more attractive to the female; (iii) Insects with mimetic females. This case is filled with examples of the first two groups, examples of the third finding places in two other cases of the series, one of which is not yet ready for exhibition.

(5) Warning colours and mimicry. As complete a series as possible of both sexes of Indian mimics of different species of the brightly coloured distasteful genus Danais, each with some allied non-mimetic species beside it for comparison, forms the principal exhibit in this case. One of the most remarkable of these mimics is the female of *Euploea mulciber* (Cramer); for the colouration typical of the genus Euploea, which is retained by the male of this species, is itself mimicked by other insects, some of which are shown. In one of these, *Elymnias malelas* (Hewitson), the male resembles a Euploea, while the female, like that of *E. mulciber* has developed the Danais pattern. A few insects and arachnids mimetic of stinging Hymenoptera are also shown.

It is hoped that this series of cases will be completed before long by a case of insects illustrating concealing colouration, and one illustrating continuous and discontinuous variation, the formation of local races, etc.

Exh. XXXII. Fishery Exhibits.

Exhibited by Mr. T. Southwell, Fishery Department, Bengal, Bihar and Orissa.

I. CARP.

(*a*) Preserved specimens of the male and female gonads of *Labeo rohita* (Rohu).

(*b*) Eggs of *Labeo rohita* as they appear immediately after fertilization.

(*c*) Growth stages of the following up to one year :—

Labeo rohita.
Labeo calbasu.
Cirrhina mrigal.
Catla buchanani.

II. PRINCIPAL PREDATORY FISH WHICH LIVE IN TANKS AND RIVERS.

III. COPEPODA COLLECTED FROM TANKS.

These are to be found in nearly all tanks. As they die, they fall to the bottm of the tank and disintegrate. Amongst other things Carp eat mud, and extract from it this organic material.

IV. APPARATUS USED FOR ARTIFICIAL CULTIVATION OF HILSA.

The eggs from ripe Hilsa (*Clupea ilisha*) are squeezed from the abdomen of the fish into a clean basin. The milt from male hilsa is squeezed from the abdomen on to the eggs. Fertilization then takes place. The eggs are then hatched in the jars shown. The process occupies about nine days. In 1897 from three Fishery stations in America alone, 205,000,000 eggs were obtained in this way, and from this number 134,546,000 young fish were actually hatched. The pump for producing the necessary current is not shown in this exhibit. The habits of the hilsa are similar to those of the English salmon

V. FISH DISEASES.

(*a*) A larval Cestode (LIGULA SIMPLICISSIMA) from the body cavity of *Labeo rohita*. This larva may attain a length of 3 feet. In India it usually occurs in carp. It is always found in the body cavity, and is by no means rare. It is said that a few years back the carp brought to Calcutta market, were so badly infected that people refused to buy them. The parasite is sold in the markets at Marseilles as "*Ver Blanc*" and is eaten. In Italy it is known and sold as "*Maccaroni piatti.*"

In Bengal, deaths due to this parasite are probably extensive. The adult tapeworm is found in certain fish-eating birds. Eggs from the adult worm are passed with the faeces of the bird, and these, dropping into the tank (or being washed in during the rains), re-infect the fish. In tanks where there is no running water, the disease thus tends to be cumulative, although this is not the case in rivers.

(*b*) Two Cestode parasites, viz. OPHRYOCOTYLE BENGALENSIS, Southwell, and BOTHRIOCEPHALUS (ANCHESTROCEPHALUS) POLYPTERI, Leyden.

Microscopic preparations. These are of scientific interest because they are the only two Cestode parasites recorded from bony fish in India.

(c) A selection of Trematode parasites from Freshwater fish. Microscopic preparations.

1. ISOPARORCHIS TRISIMILITUBIS, Southwell.—This lives in

the air bladder of *Wallago attu* (Boali). It is believed that a younger stage of this parasite may occur in the flesh of the Mahseer (*Barbus tor*).

2. Distomum sp.—This is a larval form, parasitic on the eggs of the "Perch" *Nandus marmoratus*, common in the Ganges. The parasite destroys 10% of the eggs in situ.

3. Larval forms from *Ophiocephalus striatus* (Sol.)

(*d*) Parasitic Copepoda from the body and gills of Bengal Carp.

Microscopic preparations.—This parasite produces profound Anaemia amongst the fish attacked, and deaths are very frequent. It has been found that the presence of frogs in tanks tends to keep down the disease and if upright bamboos are fixed in the tank the fish frequently rub themselves free.

(*e*) Various species of fish with skin disease. These latter consist of small nodules the size of a pins-head. They appear to be of two colours, black and white. The disease has not yet been identified. It appears to consist of a sac, full of spores. In America a similar disease is prevalent, and the mortality is high. The deaths in those cases are due, not to the "spores," if they be such, but to the growth of the fungus *Saprolegnia ferax* in the wound, when the sac ruptures. The mycelium of this fungus ramifies through the body and eventually kills the fish.

Exh. XXXIII. Original drawings of Indian Fish and Invertebrates.

Exhibited by S. C. Mondul, A. C. Chowdhary and D. N. Bagchi.

These drawings were prepared from specimens in the Museum, some of which are also exhibited, mostly for reproduction in the "Illustrations of the Zoology of the R.I.M.S.S. Investigator," in the various monographs on marine zoology published by the Trustees, or in the "Records," and "Memoirs of the Indian Museum."

The following are the subjects of the drawings :—

1. Indian deep-sea Fish and Crustacea—by S. C. Mondul.
2. Indian freshwater Fish, Fruit-flies and Frogs—by A. C. Chowdhary.
3. Indian Insects—by D. N. Bagchi.

Calcutta :—Printed at the Baptist Mission Press.